Clandestine Marriages in the Chapel and Rules of the Fleet Prison 1680–1754 Volume 2

Mark Herber is a solicitor who specialises in fraud investigations. He is a member of the Society of Genealogists and has been tracing his family tree since 1979. He is also the author of *Ancestral Trails – the complete guide to British genealogy and family history* – which was published in 1997 by Sutton Publishing in association with the Society of Genealogists. This was awarded the 1997 Library Association McColvin Medal for an outstanding work of reference.

Mark Herber

Clandestine Marriages in the Chapel and Rules of the Fleet Prison 1680–1754
Volume 2

Transcripts of registers and a notebook at the Public Record Office;
Piece RG 7/3; 1678 to 1679, 1707 to 1709, 1728 to 1729
Piece RG 7/163; 1737 to 1740
Piece RG 7/563; 1726, 1728 and 1730

Francis
Boutle
Publishers

First published by Francis Boutle Publishers
23 Arlington Way
London EC1R 1UY
(0171) 278 4497

ISBN 0 9532388 4 9

Printed in Great Britain by Redwood Books

Acknowledgements

I have been interested in the Fleet marriages for many years, but it was only in late 1995 that I had the opportunity to begin a detailed study of the surviving Fleet Registers. My original plan was to transcribe as many of the registers as possible and find a publisher willing to bring these important records to the attention of a wider public.

The vast number of registers, the difficulty of reading and transcribing many of the entries, and the commercial uncertainties and cost of publication, have sometimes caused me to doubt the wisdom of my plan. I therefore have to thank John Titford for his repeated expressions of enthusiasm and support over the years. I must also thank Clive Boutle for his interest in the project and his agreement to publish this series of books.

I must also thank the staff at the Public Record Office and the Family Records Centre, who have always dealt with my requests for registers or photocopies with such speed and efficiency – particularly important when many of my visits to the old Chancery Lane offices were limited to one hour at lunchtime.

I would like to record my gratitude for the kind and encouraging words of those who reviewed the first volume in this series, and I would also like to thank the many people who bought it. I hope this second volume is as well received.

Finally, I have to thank Colleen Keck for her continued support of my work and I therefore dedicate this volume to her.

Mark Herber
April 1999.

Contents

List of illustrations

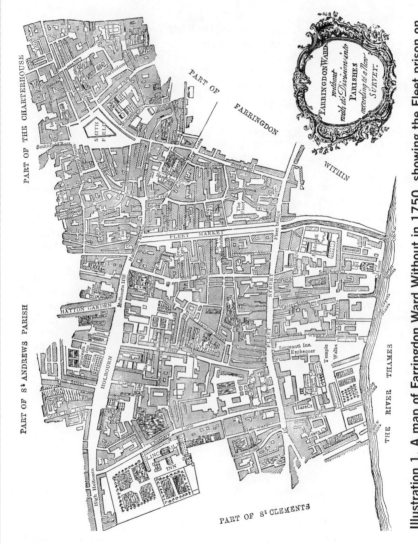

Illustration 1. A map of Farringdon Ward Without in 1750, showing the Fleet prison on the east side of Fleet market.

The Fleet registers

Since the thirteenth century the Church has laid down rules for couples who asked it to marry them. If a couple could not comply with these rules, or for some reason did not wish to, they could be married in an irregular marriage ceremony. These were treated as valid by the English courts despite the failure to observe the Church rules. Irregular marriages might also have an element of secrecy; these were known as clandestine marriages, and were also recognised as legally valid.

Irregular and clandestine marriages took place from the thirteenth century but were most popular and commonplace following the Restoration of 1660 until 1754, when the law was changed to require all marriages to conform to the rules of the Church of England. The records of irregular and clandestine marriages are of great importance to anyone undertaking genealogical research.

The trade in clandestine and irregular marriages boomed in London in the seventeenth century at churches such as Holy Trinity, Minories and St James's, Duke's Place. It continued at chapels (e.g. May Fair chapel) and also in, or near, London prisons such as the Fleet and the King's Bench prison in Southwark.

The Fleet prison, on Farringdon Street, was established in the twelfth century but, after 1655, it was primarily used to confine debtors and those in contempt of court. There were too many inmates for the prison to hold and many were permitted to reside in the Rules (or Liberties) of the Fleet, a congested, lawless area outside the prison bounded by Ludgate Hill, Old Bailey, Farringdon Street and Fleet Lane. It is shown in the map at illustration 1 (opposite), on the east side of Fleet market, later Farringdon Street. The Fleet remained a prison until its closure in 1842 but, from about 1700 until 1754, the prison and the Rules were also the most famous (or infamous) centre for clandestine marriage in England.

Clandestine marriages were conducted by priests in the Fleet prison chapel and later in chapels, marriage houses and taverns that were established in the Rules. Many of the marriages (and some baptisms) were recorded in registers and notebooks by the priests, clerks and the keepers of the marriage houses. These registers and notebooks are known collectively as the Fleet Registers.

The registers were held in private hands until 1821, when most of the present collection was purchased by the Government and then held by the Bishop of London. A few further registers were located and the whole collection was transferred to the Registrar General and later deposited at the Public Record Office (PRO) which is now at Kew. One other register is held in the Bodleian Library in Oxford.

The Fleet Registers record about 250,000 marriages as having taken place between 1690 and 1754. This is a substantial proportion of all the marriages that took place in England in this period. It has been estimated that, during the 1740s, up to 6,600 marriages a year were taking place in the Fleet, out of an annual average of about 47,000 marriages in England. The people who married at the Fleet came from all over England and even further afield, but the majority were from London and the counties of Middlesex, Kent, Essex, Hertfordshire, Buckinghamshire, Berkshire, Surrey and Sussex. That is why the Fleet Registers are such an important source of information to genealogists and to historians.

All records at the PRO are divided into classes with unique codes. The Fleet Registers at the PRO are held with the archives of the Registrar General in class RG 7, except for two registers that are held with probate records, in class PROB 18. The registers in class RG 7 have been microfilmed and may be viewed at Kew or the PRO searchroom at the Family Records Centre, 1 Myddelton Street, London, EC1R 1UW. Each class is divided into pieces (a piece may consist of only one document, but may include a number of volumes) and each piece is identified by a piece number, such as RG 7/1 or RG 7/2. The Fleet Registers consist of 275 registers (pieces RG 7/1 to RG 7/273 and piece PROB 18/50) and more than 540 notebooks (pieces RG 7/291 to RG 7/833), as well as some loose indexes (pieces RG 7/274 to RG 7/290). Some of the registers actually consist of two or more original registers (or parts of registers) that have been bound together since their purchase in 1821.

Many of the registers are extremely large and record thousands of marriages. Even the smaller registers contain hundreds of entries and may cover a few months or a few years. Most of the registers have entries in chronological order. None of them have proper indexes. Many are indexed by way of alphabets, but these are merely lists of surnames (or sometimes just Christian names) arranged in order of their first letter, but not in strict alphabetical order. Most of the alphabets list only the names of the grooms; very few name the brides. If you know the name of a groom, you can search a few registers for him fairly quickly. However, there are so many registers and notebooks (and so many of them have no alphabets) that it is really a matter of luck if you are able to locate an ancestor in the registers.

The first person to review the Fleet Registers and publish his findings (in 1833) was John Burn. An expanded second edition of his work was published in 1834[1]. Burn included some interesting entries that he found in the registers, but he extracted only a few entries from any particular register and he included some marriages from one register that has now been shown to be a forgery.

Some later authors of general works on London combined information from Burn's work with their own research on the Fleet Prison and the local area[2], but very little additional information from the Fleet Registers is contained in these works. Further research on the registers did not take place until recent years (the work undertaken by Hale, Brown and Lloyd is noted below). More recently, important studies that review the institution of marriage since the sixteenth century and particularly the availability of clandestine ceremonies at the Fleet and elsewhere have been published[3]. Interest in genealogy has also increased and many Anglican parish registers of baptisms, marriages and burials, as well as non-parochial and non-conformist registers, have been transcribed and published. Unfortunately, this transcription work has included only a few entries from the Fleet Registers. The transcription and publication of them is therefore long overdue.

The marriage laws

The church originally regarded as valid a marriage that was created by the exchange of wedding vows between two people who were free to marry each other. From the thirteenth century, some formalities were introduced by the church authorities. By 1604, ecclesiastical law required marriages to take place in the parish church of one of the spouses, after banns had been read, or a marriage licence had been issued. People under the age of twenty-one had to obtain the consent of their parents or guardians in order to marry. Marriages should have been celebrated during the canonical hours of 8 a.m. to noon and not during certain closed seasons. The rules were codified in the ecclesiastical canons of 1604. If these canons were not complied with, the church deemed the marriage invalid.

The calling of banns was instituted in 1215. Banns are notices, proclaimed in church, of a couple's intention to get married. They are called on three of the Sundays before the wedding, in the church in which the wedding is to take place and provide an opportunity for anyone to declare any impediment to the bride and groom getting married. Banns were generally not recorded until the eighteenth century but, since then, they appear in marriage registers or in separate registers of banns.

Marriage by licence, which authorised a couple to marry without banns being proclaimed, was introduced in the fourteenth century. A marriage could take place almost immediately after the licence had been obtained, but was usually held on the following day.

There were many reasons why people preferred marriage by licence. A couple or their families might wish to avoid the publicity of banns in the parish church. They might also want to avoid waiting three weeks before the marriage could take place. Speed might have been important; perhaps because the bride was pregnant or the groom was going abroad with the Army or Navy. Licences cost more money than banns, and many who could afford the fee therefore regarded marriage by licence as a status symbol.

Marriage licences could be issued by archbishops, bishops, some archdeacons, deans and chapters, incumbents of some parishes (usually peculiars – i.e. not subject to the authority of the bishop in whose diocese they lay) or officials entitled to act on behalf of these clergymen and known as surrogates. There were two types of licence. A special licence allowed a marriage to take place anywhere, but could be granted only by the Archbishop of Canterbury (or his officials). In contrast, a common licence usually specified one or two parishes for the wedding, since the Church required a marriage to take place in the home parish of one of the spouses. In practice, however, common licences were often used at churches other than those named.

A common marriage licence could be obtained from the church official who had jurisdiction over the parishes in which the couple were resident and the parish in which they wished to marry. The licences that an archdeacon could issue were restricted to those authorising the marriages of couples living in his archdeaconry who wished to marry in a parish in the archdeaconry. If that was too restrictive to meet the couples' requirements, they would have to approach a bishop or his officials, who could grant licences for a wedding in a parish anywhere in his diocese provided, again, that the couple were residents of that diocese.

If the couple lived in different dioceses, a licence had to be obtained from the office of the Archbishop who had jurisdiction over both dioceses – Canterbury or York, as the case may be. These licences were known as Vicar-General licences because they were issued by the Archbishop's Vicar-General. If the couple lived in different ecclesiastical provinces (one in that of Canterbury and the other in York) a Faculty Office licence had to be obtained from the Master of Faculties of the Archbishop of Canterbury.

Many church authorities had jurisdiction to issue marriage licences to people living in or near London. Both the City of London and the County of Middlesex were in the Diocese of London and so licences could be obtained from the Bishop of London. However, the Archdeacon of London and the Dean and Chapters of St Paul's Cathedral and Westminster Abbey also had jurisdiction over some London parishes. Marriage licences were also granted by the Archdeacon of Middlesex and by officials of the peculiars of St Katherine by the Tower or the Deanery of the Arches.

Surrey and Kent extended to the south bank of the Thames, so places such as Lambeth, Southwark and Deptford were in other ecclesiastical jurisdictions. Marriage licences for their inhabitants were issued by the Bishop of Winchester (for the Archdeaconry of Surrey) or officials of the Deanery of Croydon or the Bishop of Rochester (whose diocese covered west Kent). Furthermore, both the Faculty Office and the Vicar-General of the Archbishop of Canterbury had offices near St Paul's Cathedral, and so many Londoners found it convenient to apply to these offices for marriage licences, even if a licence from such high authority was not necessary. Both the Bishop of London and the Archbishop of Canterbury appear to have issued some licences for marriages in the Fleet prison chapel until 1711. The Bishop of London claimed that the Fleet prison was within his jurisdiction.

Marriage licences usually noted only the names of the spouses and officiating minister, plus the date and place of the ceremony. They were handed to the couple being married (and most have been lost). However, one of the couple (usually the groom) had to apply for a licence at a church official's registry by submitting an allegation. This was a sworn statement of the couples' names, ages, occupations, places of residence, condition (single or widowed) and intended place of marriage. It also confirmed that there was no impediment to the marriage. A bond may also have been submitted. This was a sworn statement, by the groom or friends or relatives of the couple, that there was no impediment to the marriage. It would also confirm the amount of money that they might forfeit if the marriage contravened the church canons.

Records of marriage licences issued by the Bishop of London are at Guildhall Library and the London Metropolitan Archives (LMA), whilst those granted by the Archbishop of Canterbury are at Lambeth Palace Library. Records of licences granted by most other bishops, archdeacons and peculiar courts are held by the appropriate county record office. More details of marriage licence records and notes on their location, indexes and transcripts are provided in my book *Ancestral Trails*[4] and in Gibson[5].

Irregular and clandestine marriages

Despite the church rules about weddings, a marriage was valid under English common law until 1754 if each spouse had merely expressed to the other an unconditional consent to the union. This was a binding contract that the courts would enforce. No particular words were necessary. Vows could be exchanged by a boy as young as fourteen and a girl as young as twelve. There was no need for a clergyman to perform a ceremony, for witnesses to be present, or for any record of the marriage to be made. Hardwicke's Marriage Act of 1753 required marriages after 25 March 1754 (except those of Quakers and Jews) to be in accordance with the church canons in order to be valid under English law. In particular the ceremony had to take place in a parish church, after banns were called or a licence obtained and be recorded in the parish register.

Before 1754, marriages that were valid under English common law, but did not comply with ecclesiastical law, were known as irregular or clandestine marriages. Steel[6], Benton[7] and Outhwaite[8] provide detailed studies of irregular and clandestine marriage, and Stone[9] is a detailed work on marriage and divorce since 1530. Marriages that took place away from the home parishes of the spouses, but after banns or a licence, were termed irregular, as were those marriages that were solemnised in the home parish of one of the spouses, but without banns or a licence. Marriages were also irregular if they were performed by clergy at an improper time.

The term clandestine is applied to those irregular weddings that also had an element of secrecy – i.e. marriages that took place away from the parties' homes and without either banns or a marriage licence. Secrecy might be desirable to one, or both, of the spouses for various reasons. A man might wish to marry an heiress without her parents' consent. A clandestine ceremony allowed the couple to present a fait accompli. Apprentices might wish to marry before the expiry of their seven-year term – a breach of their articles that they might want to keep secret. Many widows were left money by their husbands on condition that they did not remarry. A clandestine ceremony allowed them to obtain a new husband yet keep their first husband's money. A man who had deserted his wife and was remarrying bigamously preferred a clandestine ceremony even if he was miles from his old home. Clandestine marriages also had advantages of speed. They could take place almost immediately. This appealed to sailors or soldiers going abroad, or pregnant women.

Many clergymen were willing to conduct irregular or clandestine ceremonies for a suitable fee. The church authorities took action in the church courts against priests who ignored the church canons when conducting ceremonies or granting licences, but court action was sporadic and half-hearted compared to the extent of the abuses. For example, it remained easy for couples to obtain marriage licences from many surrogates, without complying with the rules as to residence in the parish in which they were to marry. Stone[10] notes that, in 1752, there were 31 surrogates of the Bishop of Worcester (in and around Worcestershire) who had authority to issue marriage licences. Many surrogates were more interested in their fees than in the true residence or age of applicants.

The number of irregular and clandestine marriages was enormous and certain churches were important centres of this trade. The chapel at the Tower of London was a clandestine-marriage centre as early as 1630. Between 1676 and 1683, almost half of all London weddings were taking place at Holy Trinity, Minories or St James's, Duke's Place. The incumbents of St James's, Duke's Place claimed to be exempt from control of the church authorities because they were appointed by the

Lord Mayor and citizens of London rather than the Church. The parishioners of Holy Trinity, Minories had the right to appoint their minister. These clergymen could ignore the church authorities and canon law and increase their income by marrying whomever they wished.

The Marriage Duty Acts of 1694 and 1695 required that places 'pretending to be exempt from the visitation of the Bishop of the Diocese', that is, the centres of the irregular and clandestine marriage trade, should conduct marriages only after the calling of banns or the obtaining of a licence. A clergyman who ignored this requirement could be fined £100. However, the incumbents of many London churches were then appointed as surrogates by the Bishop of London and issued the marriage licences required by couples. Couples also continued to obtain licences from the London offices of the Vicar-General or Faculty Office of the Archbishop of Canterbury.

Furthermore, whilst the £100 fine resulted in a decline in irregular marriages at some churches, it also led to increased business for clergy who were not perturbed by a fine – those imprisoned for debt for instance. The Fleet therefore became important from this time as a clandestine marriage centre. By the 1740s, more than half of all London weddings were taking place there. Marriages were also performed at the King's Bench prison in Southwark and in the surrounding area (known as the Mint), which was a place of refuge for debtors and thieves. The Reverend Alexander Keith also ignored the legislation – his May Fair Chapel was built in 1729, near to the parish church of St George, Hanover Square. He conducted hundreds of irregular marriages until he was excommunicated in 1742 and imprisoned in the Fleet[11]

Most weddings at London marriage centres were of couples from London (or nearby counties), but many came from other parts of Britain. Irregular marriages did not take place only in London. Registers of parishes throughout England include many marriages of couples (with a licence) who were not resident there. These parishes were often near the seat of a bishop or surrogate who could issue licences. The minister of the parish of Fledborough in Nottinghamshire was appointed as a surrogate in 1730 and he then issued many licences and married many couples. Only eleven marriages took place in the parish from 1712 to 1730, but from 1730 to 1754 there were 490, only fifteen of the couples residing in the village.

The surviving registers of the most important London marriage centres – i.e. St Pancras; St James's, Duke's Place; St Dunstan, Stepney; St Benet, Paul's Wharf; St Gregory by St Paul; Holy Trinity, Minories; St Katherine by the Tower and St Botolph, Aldgate – are at Guildhall Library and the LMA. Some of these registers have been published[12]. The registers of Keith's May Fair Chapel have also been published[13]. Surviving registers from the King's Bench Prison and Mint are at the PRO (with the Fleet registers in class RG 7). However, many important registers have not survived. Some registers of Holy Trinity, Minories (from 1649 to 1658 and from 1663 to 1676) are missing, as are the registers of St James's, Duke's Place for 1668 to 1679. Many Fleet and King's Bench registers have also been lost.

The end of clandestine marriages

The clandestine and irregular marriage trade in England and Wales was brought to an end by Hardwicke's Marriage Act. This required all marriages, except Jewish or

Illustration 2. An engraving of one of the courtyards in the Fleet prison

Quaker ceremonies, to take place in the parish church of one of the spouses, during canonical hours, after banns, or with a licence, in which case one of the spouses had to have been resident in the parish for four weeks. The act stipulated that marriage registers should be kept, with signatures or marks of the parties and witnesses. Marriages that did not comply with the act were void. Any minister conducting such a marriage was guilty of a felony and could be transported.[14] Couples who wanted a secret ceremony had to travel to Scotland or the Channel Islands, where Hardwicke's Act did not apply.

The Fleet prison

The Fleet prison had a chapel and its own chaplain to serve the inmates for worship. Marriages were also conducted in the chapel from at least the early seventeenth century. However, the Fleet Chapel became a centre for clandestine marriages only around 1680 and it was only in 1696, after the Marriage Acts, that it flourished (as other marriage centres declined). As a prison, the Fleet was, or was claimed to be, outside the jurisdiction of the church authorities. Anyone could visit the prison and the inmates included some clergymen who were willing to marry anyone in the prison chapel for a fee (shared with the prison wardens). The number of marriages in the chapel gradually increased until the authorities moved to stamp out this abuse. An act of 1711 imposed fines on prison keepers for permitting marriages to be performed in prison chapels without banns or licences.

However, the clandestine marriage trade simply moved outside the prison walls. Many indebted clergymen lived in the Rules of the Fleet and many other disgraced or crooked clergymen (or charlatans pretending to be clergy) sheltered there, relatively safe from the authorities. Chapels and marriage houses were set up in the Rules, many in taverns (a few were actually outside the Rules[15]) and the marriage business continued despite the 1711 act. The success of the trade attracted other clergymen to the Rules, keen to make money by conducting simple marriage ceremonies, even though they were breaking the church canons. Some of the parsons also conducted marriages at their own homes, even if they lived outside the Rules; some visited private homes in London or elsewhere and recorded these marriages in the registers and notebooks.

Many people believe that most Fleet weddings involved a young heiress marrying an unsuitable rake without the consent of her parents. There were undoubtedly some marriages of this type, but the majority of couples appear to have used the Fleet or other clandestine marriage centres to save money. Anglican clergy charged fees not only for a wedding ceremony, but also for calling banns or issuing a licence. The Fleet parsons charged lower fees (the fees are sometimes noted in the registers). Furthermore, a marriage often involved an expensive wedding feast, with many friends and relatives invited for food, drink and entertainment. However, only a few close friends and relatives need be invited to a Fleet wedding – and sometimes there would be no guests whatsoever.

The Fleet Registers also contain some records of baptisms. Many are baptisms of adults described as negro or black. I do not know why these baptisms took place at the Fleet, but it may have been that many parish clergy were unwilling to conduct these ceremonies.

The Fleet was not merely a marriage centre for criminals and the poor, a wide range of people, rich and poor, married there – gentlemen, craftsmen (such as shoe or wig makers, silversmiths and carpenters), mariners, servants, farmers, labourers, soldiers or inn-keepers. It was a particularly popular marriage centre for sailors.

A number of entries in the registers refer to the groom as a gentleman. However, this may have been a very loose use of the term and it is unlikely that many people who were truly upper or middle class used the Fleet. The Fleet enabled a couple to have a ceremony away from the prying eyes of the public, or friends and relatives, but if privacy were the object, it could be achieved by marrying by licence. Some of the upper classes did marry in the Fleet or arrange for a Fleet parson to visit their home. Roger Brown studied the Fleet Register entries for certain years and wrote a thesis[16] about the registers and parsons. He discovered an entry for the marriage of Colonel William Peirs, who was the Member of Parliament for Wells in Somerset, and also an entry for the marriage of Lady Catherine Annisley of Buckinghamshire.

Unlike Anglican parishes (or other clandestine centres), the Fleet had many ministers conducting marriages at any one time – more than seventy parsons were working in the prison or Rules between 1700 and 1753. Burn[17] included short biographies of the known ministers, and he also listed some of the men who kept the marriage houses and registers. Further information about them was included by Brown in his thesis.

Most of the clergymen were poor – some had lost their benefices for matrimonial or other offences – and were no doubt attracted by the money to be made from marriage ceremonies in the Fleet. Most of the marriage-house keepers owned taverns or alehouses and provided a room as a chapel in which the parsons could conduct ceremonies.

Many of the parsons kept notebooks in which they noted the marriages that they conducted. Most of these entries were then copied into registers. Some registers were held and completed by the parsons (or clerks paid by them) and some by the marriage-house keepers.

There were also many clerks who prepared registers by copying as many entries as they could find in other registers.These compilations record ceremonies performed by various ministers at different marriage houses. The ministers or register keepers might issue certificates to couples who married in the Fleet and, since many people later wanted evidence of a marriage, they charged further fees for conducting searches in the registers. A marriage might therefore be recorded three times or even more – by a minister in his notebook and register, by the marriage house keeper and also by a register keeper.

The registers and notebooks therefore overlap in time and many marriages appear in more than one register or notebook. The surviving registers and notebooks record only a few marriages before 1700, so that some of the earlier registers appear to be missing. Many later registers and notebooks have also been lost or destroyed. It is therefore difficult to estimate how many people married in the Fleet. I estimate that the surviving registers and notebooks contain approximately 350,000 entries, but thousands of these entries duplicate others. The duplicate entries often contain differences because of transcription errors at the time of copying. These errors might relate to the date, the couples' names, their occupations or place of residence.

The entries in the registers and notebooks were in a form similar to that of parish registers, as can be seen from illustration 3 (opposite), a page from the register in piece RG 7/116, with entries from 1–3 May 1731. Most of the registers contain entries in roughly chronological order, but some are in the form of alphabets, with the entries arranged by the first letter of the groom's surname. Many Fleet Registers are superior to pre-1754 parish registers, since most entries note the parish of each spouse and the groom's occupation. In illustration 3, three grooms are cordwainers, one a skinner, one a sailor, one a drayman (the other was noted as a gentleman).

Most marriages in the Fleet were between couples living in London or nearby counties, but people came from all over England (and sometimes the rest of Britain or the colonies). Most of the spouses recorded in the entries in illustration 3 were from London or Middlesex parishes, but Thomas Goodman was from Greenwich, in Kent, and John Rouse was from Cambridge. As further examples of couples from outside London, here are two entries of December 1726 from a small register in piece RG 7/98:

11th. George Pope, weaver of the parish of Crediton in Devonshire and Temperance Courtenay of Colebrook in Devonshire (a bachelor and spinster)

14th. Robert Hutson, seafaring man of Scarborough in Yorkshire and Mary O'Brian, widow

As already mentioned, the availability of cheap, clandestine ceremonies at the Fleet resulted in many abuses. For example, many grooms and brides were minors who were getting married without their parents' consent. A couple might also seek a clandestine ceremony because they were within the prohibited degrees and forbidden by ecclesiastical law from marrying. For instance, the rules prohibited marriages between a brother and sister, or even between a man and his brother's widow. Such a couple could marry at the Fleet with little fear of detection.

Many entries in the Fleet Registers record spouses with the same surname and they are often noted as widowed. Some genealogical research should be carried out in respect of particular entries, but it is very likely that some of these couples were within the prohibited degrees, for example, a man marrying the sister of his deceased wife or the widow of his deceased brother. It is even possible that some entries concern marriages of a brother and sister. The abuses are sometimes recorded in the registers and many entries note that the marriage must be kept secret. I have found an entry stating that a widow would lose her jointure – her share in the estate left by her husband – if the marriage became known. Burn[18] found an entry recording that the groom was later discovered to be a woman and another entry[19] noting that the bride had a husband who was still alive.

The dates of marriages were sometimes changed at the request of the couple, for example, so that the marriage would appear to pre-date the birth of a child by more than nine months. Some entries, recording perhaps the wedding of an heiress to a fortune-seeker, or the eldest son of a wealthy family to an unsuitable girl, were altered or erased, perhaps after a payment to the parson or clerk by distressed parents. The Fleet parsons might record the date of a marriage in the registers or notebooks but provide the couple with a certificate of the marriage with a false date –

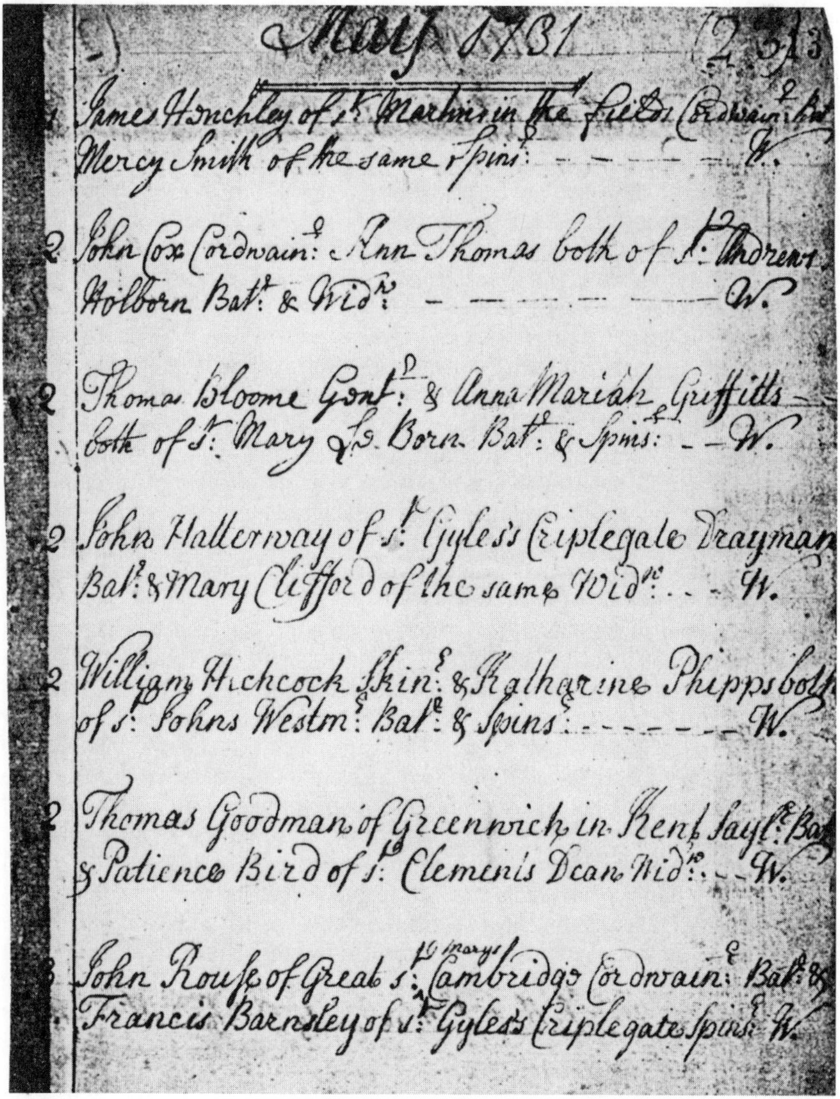

Illustration 3. A page (folio 13 recto) from the register in piece **RG 7/116**; marriages of 1–3 May 1731

an attractive option for a couple who already had a child.

Furthermore, a few entries in the registers were fictitious and some forgeries are noted in the studies by Burn, Lloyd, Outhwaite and Stone. The Fleet Registers must, therefore, be used with caution.

However, most marriages at the Fleet simply involved a man and a woman who wished to be married quickly and cheaply. The Fleet Registers are not only important to those who have London ancestors who were very poor or even criminals. People of all classes and occupations married in the Fleet. The entries concern soldiers, artisans, farmers, servants and sailors. The registers also include people from all parts of the British Isles and even from abroad. Many of us therefore have ancestors who married at the Fleet.

There are only a few transcripts and indexes of entries from the Fleet Registers. A few entries were noted by Burn (and these were incorporated into Percival Boyd's marriage index). The PRO and Society of Genealogists hold an indexed transcript, by Stephen Hale, to about 6,700 Fleet marriages. This large work does not contain any complete registers, but only extracts (entries in which one or both spouses were stated to reside in particular parishes in Sussex, Kent or Surrey) from the many registers that Hale reviewed. The Society of Genealogists also holds a transcript, by S.W. Prentis, of a notebook (piece RG 7/833 at the PRO). Unfortunately, the original writing in the notebook is difficult to decipher and the transcript contains some errors.

The only other substantial transcription work on the Fleet Registers prior to this series of books was that by Beric Lloyd[20]. Lloyd had a particular purpose, that is to show that what appeared to be one of the earliest of the Fleet Registers – presently the first of the three sections in piece RG 7/2 – was in fact a forgery. The forger had copied the 248 entries from parts of other registers, but changed the dates so that the forgery appeared to be about 60 years older than it really was (probably so that the forger could obtain a high price for it when registers were being bought and sold in the eighteenth and nineteenth centuries). Lloyd published a transcript of this forgery, and also of those entries in the two registers (RG 7/118 and RG 7/162) that the forger had used to create the 248 forged entries in RG 7/2. Lloyd did not therefore publish the vast majority of entries contained in RG 7/118 and RG 7/162. Consequently, I included complete versions of the two registers (336 marriages and one baptism in RG 7/118 and 921 marriages in RG 7/162) in the first volume of this series, the first time that any complete Fleet Registers had been published. The present volume includes two more registers (RG 7/3 and RG 7/163) and a notebook (RG 7/563). It is intended to publish many more and make them available to a wider audience.

The register in RG 7/3 contains 719 marriages (and six baptisms) with the earliest dated November 1678 and the latest December 1729. It is likely that the entries of 1678 and 1679 were copied from other registers or notebooks and given these false dates. Many of the marriages of 1728 were performed by John Floud (or Floyd), and I located one of his notebooks (RG 7/563) containing his original records of many of these ceremonies. I have therefore included it in this volume. I have also included the register in RG 7/163 which records 119 marriages performed by Walter Wyatt, one of the most successful of the Fleet ministers. These marriages were apparently to be kept secret. Seventy-eight of the grooms are noted as being gentlemen (one of them a baronet) and Wyatt records that he issued back-dated certificates to nine of the marriages.

Notes on the registers

The entries that appear on the following pages are exact transcripts (RG 7/3 and RG 7/563) or abstracts of the important information from each entry (RG 7/163). In the introduction to each register, I have drawn the attention of the reader to entries of particular interest or to entries that illustrate the use of the Fleet by particular types of people.

I have retained the original spelling of words in the registers and presented the surnames of the spouses in capital letters to help the reader locate entries, but I have otherwise followed the writers' use of capital letters and punctuation, inconsistent though this often is. For example, the name of a church may appear with capitals in one entry, but lower case letters in the following one. There are many words that have clearly been incorrectly spelt, but which can be easily identified, for example, the names of counties and some places. Many of the names of the brides and grooms have no doubt also been incorrectly spelt. However, I have not attempted to correct the spelling of these, even in those cases where the true name is fairly obvious, but I have made some suggestions in the notes to many entries and the suggested surnames are also indexed.

I have also transcribed the dates of the entries exactly as they appear in the original registers. Some entries have complete dates (e.g. 8 October 1743), but others simply note the date of the month. In these cases, the full date of the entry can be found by referring to previous entries, particularly the last entry to include the month and year. However, caution must be exercised in respect of some entries that were inserted in the registers, particularly those entries in a different hand. The true date of these marriages is uncertain.

My notes or comments on the entries are in italics and contained in square brackets at the end of each entry. If the note relates to a particular word or figure in an entry, that is indicated by the sign * at the relevant point in the entry. If an entry is contained in both RG 7/3 and RG 7/563, the entry number for the other is included in the notes.

The register in RG 7/3 and notebook in RG 7/563 illustrate many of the problems of using the Fleet Registers. The differences between the entries contained in registers and notebooks are often substantial. The notebooks commonly include more information about a marriage, particularly the place within the Fleet where the marriage was conducted and also the spouses' occupations and residence. These are sometimes omitted from the registers.

The problems caused by the incorrect copying of entries from notebooks to registers and then to other registers was illustrated in volume 1 by certain entries from the registers in pieces RG 7/162 and RG 7/118. Minor spelling errors abound in many entries and the copyist who prepared the register in RG 7/162 even merged two entries into one (see entry 65 in RG 7/162 and entries 68 and 69 in RG 7/118), noting the groom from one entry, and the bride from the next. Mistakes in copying were quite extreme on some occasions as the following three entries, from a notebook in piece RG 7/497, and the registers in RG 7/118 and RG 7/162, reveal:

RG 7/497
Wm. TYATH of St Sepulchers tin plate worker & widr and Mary RESTE of do.
Spr

RG 7/118
————— —————— tin man & Mary RESTE

RG 7/162
————— LINMAN & Mary RESTE

In this way, William TYATH, a tin plate worker, became just an unnamed tin man and then a man surnamed LINMAN, but without an occupation. In this volume I have noted the errors that were made when entries from RG 7/563 were copied into RG 7/3. It is therefore vital, if you find an ancestor in the Fleet Registers, to consult other registers and the parsons' notebooks covering the same period, in order to locate and compare other versions of the entry.

Researchers who have used parish registers will find it easy to use these transcripts of the Fleet Registers; indeed, many entries in the Fleet Registers are superior to those in some parish registers. The information is usually set out in a standard fashion: a date, the names of the couple, their places of residence and the occupation of the groom. The condition of each spouse is usually noted and this reveals that, at the Fleet, widows and widowers constituted a surprisingly high proportion of those marrying. Most entries also feature the name of the minister who conducted the ceremony, and some entries (particularly in the notebooks) include notes of the fees paid. A few entries have notes about the spouses that were added by the ministers or the clerks. As noted above, these can be illuminating.

As with parish registers, many abbreviations were used. The spouses' conditions were usually expressed as B, Bat or Br for a bachelor; as S, Sp or Spin for a spinster; and as W, Ww, Wid or Widr for a widow or widower. An occupation may have been abbreviated, for example, cord for cordwainer or Husb for husbandman. Some abbreviations cause difficulty. An entry may, for instance, identify the minister only by an abbreviation. The minister may be identifiable from other entries or notes in the register, or from entries contained in the ministers' notebooks. However, this is not always possible and assumptions should not be made. In particular, an entry that ends with W may have been a marriage conducted by Dr Wyatt; but it may simply indicate that the bride was a widow.

At the end of this book is a surname index and an index to places. The surname index refers to the spouses named in the two registers and the notebook, and to those mentioned in the notes to each entry.

The index to places includes counties, and countries other than England. Middlesex and the City of London have been excluded because the majority of entries relate to them. The index refers to a county only if it is specifically mentioned in the entry – which is often the case – or in my notes, or if a spouse's residence is a town or city where the name is the same, or similar to, the name of the county. A spouse resident in Cambridge or Bedford, for example, would appear in the index under Cambridgeshire and Bedfordshire respectively.

Notes

1   J.S. Burn; *History of the Fleet Marriages; with some account of the Wardens of the Prison, the Parsons, and their Registers: to which are added notices of the May Fair, Mint and Savoy Chapels and numerous extracts from the registers*; Rivington, 2nd ed. (1834).
2   The most interesting is John Ashton; *The Fleet, its river, prison and marriages*, T. Fisher Unwin (1889)
3   Particularly works by Outhwaite and Stone, noted below.
4   *Ancestral trails; the complete guide to British genealogy and family history*; Sutton Publishing (1997)
5   J. Gibson; *Bishops' transcripts and marriage licences, bonds and allegations; a guide to their location and indexes*; FFHS, 4th ed. (1997)
6   D.J. Steel & A.E.F. Steel; *National index of parish registers, volume I, sources of births, marriages and deaths before 1837*; Society of Genealogists (1968)
7   A.Benton; *Irregular Marriage in London before 1754*; Society of Genealogists (1993)
8   R.B. Outhwaite; *Clandestine marriage in England 1500–1850*; Hambledon Press (1995)
9   L. Stone; *Road to divorce, England 1530–1837*; OUP (1992)
10 Stone; op. cit. p 102
11 However, Keith had also established a chapel in a house in Mayfair and appointed curates who continued to conduct marriages on his behalf whilst he was in prison.
12 For example, East of London FHS has published microfiche indexes to the marriage registers of Holy Trinity, Minories (1676 to 1754); see also W.P.W. Phillimore and G.E. Cokayne; *Marriages at St James Duke's Place, London 1665–1837*; Phillimore (1900–2).
13 G.J. Armytage; *The registers of baptisms and marriages at St George's chapel, May Fair*; Harleian Society (1889).
14 The minister at the Savoy Chapel in London conducted irregular marriages for more than 1,500 couples in 1754 and 1755. He was convicted and sentenced to transportation.
15 Steel; op. cit. p298
16 R.L. Brown; *Clandestine marriages in London, especially within the Fleet Prison and their effect in Hardwicke's Act 1753*; unpublished MA thesis (1972), microfilm at Guildhall Library
17 op. cit. pp 49 and following
18 ibid. p 90
19 ibid. p 78
20 B. Lloyd; *The Fleet forgeries; a study of the crime and carelessness of the clerical classes in the days of yore*; B. Lloyd (1987).

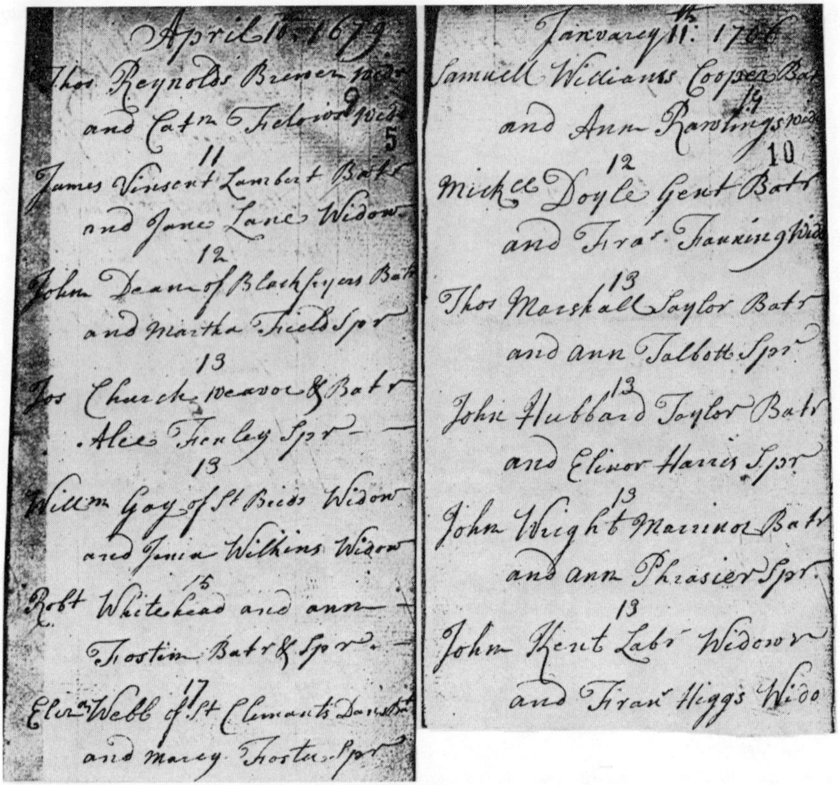

Illustration 4. Parts of two pages (folio 5 recto and folio 10 recto) from the register in piece RG 7/3; marriages of 10–17 April 1679 and 11–13 January 1706

Register of Marriages in piece RG 7/3

From November 1678 to October 1679, January 1706/7 to May 1707, August 1707, February 1708/9 to December 1709, February 1725 and August 1728 to December 1729

This register is described in the PRO class list as consisting of four parts, as follows:
   a) November 1678 to October 1679
   b) January 1707 to February 1708
   c) March 1709 to December 1709, and
   d) August 1728 to December 1729.
In fact, the entries in the register appear to cover the periods:
   a) November 1678 to October 1679 (but see later in this introduction)
   b) January 1706/7 to May 1707
   c) August 1707
   d) February 1708/9 to December 1709,
   e) February 1725 (one entry only), and
   f) August 1728 to December 1729
Piece RG 7/3 consists of a PRO binding, about 13 inches high by about 4 inches wide, surrounding a register with board covers, of about the same size. Inside these covers are 56 folios (folio 56 has become stuck to the inside back cover). Folios 43 verso and 44 verso are blank and folio 55 recto is blank apart from the words 'Decmb. 1729'. On the register's front cover, in manuscript, is '1678 1721 ?[illegible] Floyd Mottram'. There are also two white labels; on one appears '241' and on the other appears 'Fleet Marriages 176'. On the inside front cover is the following manuscript title:

Marriges Registers & Performed by Different Ministers
mr Floyd mr Mottram
the Revd mr Jones
the Revd mr Hinsen mr Cutbart
the Revd mr James Wagstaff
the Revd mr John Evans

A full transcript of this register is set out below with the addition, to assist the reader, of 'and' in square brackets just before the bride's name in entries where 'and' or '&' does not already occur. The register does not include an index and the entries are not numbered, so in this transcript I have given numbers to each entry for ease of reference. There are 725 entries in this register of which 719 are marriages and six are baptisms (entries 95, 106, 155, 357, 440 and 585). A few of the entries are repeated (for example entry 155 is repeated at entry 357), but with different dates or differences in spelling or other details.

Although many of the entries (especially those in the early parts of the register) do not name the officiating minister, a substantial number (for example entry 430 and following) are noted as performed by John Floud (or Floyd). He was usually known as Floud, or even Flood, but his name in the register is usually written as Floyd. The PRO class list notes John Floud as the officiating minister for the marriages in the section covering August 1728 to December 1729 (that is entries 430 to 725 below). This is not entirely correct. Although most of the entries include the name of Floud, Floyd (or the initials JF), some entries do not indicate the name of the officiating minister and some entries note the name of other ministers. Entries of marriages by these ministers also appear in other parts of the register. They include marriages by Pretty (entries 368, 389, 391 and 394), Jones (369, 388 and 395), Mottram (370 to 374, 382, 386 and 685) and Stacy or Stacey (674, 678, 682, 683 and 686). There are also a number of entries for marriages performed by Sanhope (365), Cuthbert (367), Wagstaff (623 and 673), Ryder (662 and 665), Evans (710) and Wigmore (711 and 714).

The large number of ministers who performed the marriages recorded in this register suggests that the register was either compiled at a marriage house (at which a number of ministers performed ceremonies) or that it was compiled by a clerk from the marriage registers or the notebooks of various ministers or marriage houses.

It does not appear to have been a register of marriages of a particular marriage house, since so many of the entries in the later parts of the register note the name of the marriage house at which the ceremony was performed. Furthermore, part of this register (entries numbered 514–516, 518–605, 607–619, 651–653, 657, 670, 723 and 725), was clearly copied from part of one of Floud's notebooks (in piece RG 7/563 and also transcribed in this volume). In entry 178 of this register, the name 'Hanah' has been crossed out and the name Marey then written. Hanah is the name of the bride in the previous entry, which suggests that a clerk was copying these entries from another source. In entries 185 and 186, the name of the bride is the same, Eliz Evins, again suggesting that the clerk was copying these entries from another source and made a mistake.

Entries 1 to 618 in this register are, in my opinion, all in the hand of the same person. This can be seen from illustration 4, which includes extracts from folio 5 recto, with entries of 10–17 April 1679 and folio 10 recto, with entries of 11–13 January 1706/7. The handwriting is the same. The jump in date occurs at the entry that I have numbered 183 (in the transcript below). Entry 182 is dated 19 October 1679 and entry 183 is dated 9 January 1706. Despite this jump of 26 years, the handwriting does not vary. Similar jumps in time occur later in the register. Entries of December 1709 end at entry 428. Entry 429 is dated 9 February 1725 and entries for August 1728 commence at entry 430. The same handwriting continues. All the entries in RG 7/3 that I have numbered 1 to 618, therefore appear to have been written by the same person, probably within a short period of time. It is only at entry 619, dated October 1728, that the previous style of handwriting ceases and the remaining entries in the register are in various hands.

In view of these factors, it is likely that most of the register (if not all of it) was copied from ministers' registers and notebooks. However, I have been unable to locate any notebooks or registers (other than RG 7/563) that were used and it is possible that the other sources were lost before the government purchased the surviving Fleet Registers.

The entries from the notebook in piece RG 7/563 were copied into this register with varying degrees of accuracy. For example, entry 26 in the notebook records the marriage of James Wood and Ann Willson on 25 September 1728. This entry has been copied into the register correctly at entry 540 but omits some detail (the groom's occupation and the place of marriage; the Black Lion in Stonecutter Street). There were some minor copying mistakes. For example, entry 30 in the notebook records the marriage of John Ellis and Anne Reich on 29 September 1728. This entry has been copied into the register at entry 544 but the bride's surname has been incorrectly copied as Rich. At the other extreme, entry 25 in the notebook records the marriage of William Thomarver, a sawyer and Jane Wakeford on 24 September 1728. This has been incorrectly copied into the register, at entry 539, as the marriage of William Sawyer. This confirms the importance of searching the notebooks, even though there are hundreds of them, to locate an entry of your ancestors' marriage that has already been found in the registers. The notebook entries are likely to be more accurate than entries that were copied into registers. Even a small error in copying the name of one of the spouses could make it impossible for a researcher to find an ancestor's marriage in the register. It is therefore all the more unfortunate that so many of the notebooks have not survived.

The clerk who copied the entries from the notebook in RG 7/563 into the register in RG 7/3 also omitted certain entries (described in the section of this book that deals with the notebook). Some of these notebook entries were clearly written into the notebook in a different hand from most of the other entries. It may be that they were only inserted into the notebook after a clerk had copied entries into the register in RG 7/3. The entries that I have numbered 107 and following in the notebook (except for the marriages at entries 156–158, 178, 180, 186, 198 and 204, and the baptism at entry 199) also do not appear in the register in piece RG 7/3. It may be that they were only entered into the notebook after the notebook had been copied into the register. Alternatively, the copyist may have taken a break after copying entry 106 into the register in RG 7/3 and then for some reason turned to another source and only copied a few more entries from the notebook that interested him.

It is also interesting that the register in RG 7/3 contains two entries (517 and 606), within the section containing the entries from the notebook, that do not appear in that notebook. Where did these entries come from? Perhaps John Floud had written them on scraps of paper (kept loose in his notebook?) that have now been lost. Maybe the clerk had another notebook, with a few entries for these dates, and he chose to insert them with the entries from this notebook. We shall probably never know.

The entries in the earliest section of this register, that is entries 1 to 182, have dates from November 1678 to October 1679. It was suggested by Beric Lloyd (see the introduction to this volume) that all the entries before 1680 in the Fleet Registers were copies of records of actual marriages, but that they been given earlier dates by the clerks who were preparing the copy registers. Lloyd only published his evidence for this statement in respect of one section of the register in RG 7/2, and the whereabouts of his working papers is not known. Lloyd may well be correct, but this will only be certain when further transcription of the registers and notebooks has been completed. However, Lloyd's suggestion is supported by evidence from this register. Entries 148, 149, 154, 155, 160 and 167 (with dates of August and September 1679) also appear at entries 353, 354, 356, 357, 358 and 359 (with dates from 16 May to 19 May 1707). Furthermore, entries 147 and 150 are very similar to entries 352 and 355 respectively (the differences may be accounted for by copying errors). In each case, one of the dates must be wrong and it seems plausible to suggest that, for each marriage, it is the earlier date that is the fabrication and the later date that is correct. In view of these known fabrications, it seems likely that many, if not all of entries 1 to 182 in this register were copied from later entries in other registers or notebooks, but given incorrect, earlier dates. The information in these entries is likely to be correct, apart from the date, and versions of these entries, with correct dates, may survive in other registers or notebooks in the collection.

It is also worth noting that entries 228, 230 and 231 in this register (dated 6 February 1706/7), are repeated at entries 346, 347 and 344 respectively, with dates in April and May 1706/7. I cannot provide any explanation for this duplication except to suggest that entries for each of the marriages appeared in more than one register or notebook (with a mistake as to the date in one), so that the clerk copied both versions into the register in RG 7/3, because he did not know which date was correct. This may also explain the duplication of some entries from 1728 and 1729. Entries 515, 516, 519, 616, 621 and 678 also appear at entries 628, 630, 706, 717, 658 and 720, but with different dates. One marriage appears three times; at entry 537 (dated 24 September 1728), entry 576 (6 October 1728) and entry 708 (August 1729).

Entry 357 (repeating entry 155) is for the baptism of an adult black man. Entry 440 is also a baptism of a black man or boy and entry 303 is the marriage of a black couple. It will be interesting to ascertain, following further work on the Fleet Registers, the number of such marriages and baptisms that took place in the Fleet. We can only speculate about the reasons, but it was likely to have been a mixture of prejudice on the part of London Anglican parish clergy and economic difficulty for the black spouses.

Spouses came from all over Britain to be married in the Fleet. The vast majority came from London or those counties, such as Essex, Kent and Surrey, which were close to London. However, family historians who are investigating their family in other English counties, or from other parts of the British Isles, will not be disappointed because this register contains many examples of spouses coming from more distant counties.

John Huggins of Iver in Buckinghamshire married Ann Langley in the Fleet in 1706/7 (see entries 231 and 344). Edward Waine, a labourer of Kentsford (probably Kempsford) in Gloucestershire married Margaret Crowser of Harksum (probably Hexham) in Northumberland at the Goat in October 1729 (entry 716). John England, a clothworker of Wakefield in Yorkshire married Elizabeth Beddall of St Brides in London, also at the Goat, in June 1729. On 16 September 1728, John Floud performed a marriage ceremony for a Welsh couple; Griffith Griffis of Montgomery and Mary Jones of Pembroke (entry 508).

This register also illustrates the wide variety of classes and occupations of the people who married in the Fleet. 'Mariners' or 'sailors' appear in many entries; see for example entries 27, 28, 54, 100, 233, 247, 308 and 621. There are also many soldiers (for example entries 188, 277, 298, 400, 517 and 609). Their regiments are sometimes recorded as in entry 400, for the marriage of Henry Trotter of the 1st Regiment of Foot Guards and his bride Mary Pratt of the parish of St James Westminster on 19 July 1709.

The entries include gentlemen, for example, William Brodix married Ann Browning on 18 April 1707, but also labourers (for example entries 4, 321 and 390). The marriages in the register include those of farmers and husbandmen (entries 111, 185, 250 and 380), and many artisans and professionals; cordwainers (entries 3, 7, 146 and 242), butchers (entries 92, 97 and 135), weavers (entries 8, 93 and 123), apothecaries (entries 369 and 398), a silversmith (entry 121), a surgeon (entry 405), a schoolmaster (entry 105), and even a jockey (entry 322).

Finally, this register notes the places of marriage, within the Fleet, for many of the entries. The Goat, for instance, was a popular venue. Stephen Muckleroy of St James Westminster and his bride Margaret married there on 2 November 1728 (see also entries 648, 672, 695, 696 and 699). There are also references to the Barley Mow (entry 657), the Golden Ball in Old Bailey (368) and the Queen's Head (674 and 685). Some of the marriage houses were known by the name of the proprietors. Henry Batten of Stepney, a mariner, married Mary Woodham at Mrs Wilson's on 11 November 1728. Other references can be found to Mott's (entries 661 and 664), Carbett's (entries 630 and 725) and to the house of Mr Clifton (entry 669).

Folio 1 recto
1.	Novr 1678. 3. Will SELBEY of St Giles in ye fields Bat & Mary NORTH Sp
2.	5. Edward SMART of St martins in ye fields Bat & Sarah MORRIS Sp
3.	Tho MATRIN of St marys Le* Bac Cord** Bat & Mary SMITH Sp
	*[*Damage to the page has resulted in the loss of the rest of this word (and the date of the entry). **Probably short for cordwainer]*

Folio 1 verso
4.	Nov 12: 1678. Wm LORDING Labor and widower and Barbari MUNCK Spr
5.	19. Thos PARKINES of St Clemant Danes Taylor Bat & Sarah MAY Sp

Folio 2 recto
6.	December 5th 1678. Jams KITE of St Giles Criplegate Taylor Bat
	& Ursula GREEN widow
7.	7. Soloman WRIGHT of Westr* Cordwinr [and] Eliz BECK of Spittlefields B & Spr
	*[*Probably short for Westminster]*
8.	Jno. CLOEBATCH Weaver & Batr and Margrett NICKOL Spr
	[This entry is undated but the layout of the page suggests that it was entered as a marriage of the same date as entry 7]
9.	Wm LOYD Labror and Widower and Barbara JACKSON Spinster
	[This entry is undated but the layout of the page suggests that it was entered as a marriage of the same date as entry 7]
10.	Richd DALTON Painter and Patience BOWYER Bat & Spr
	[This entry is undated but the layout of the page suggests that it was entered as a marriage of the same date as entry 7]
11.	10. Thos UXLEY of Deptford Batr and Marey LEEKING Widow
12.	10. George NEVILL Coachman and Bat and Ann ROYSTON Spr
13.	10. Wm HOLLAND Smith Widowr and Usley LANGLEY Spr
14.	11. John VINCENT of Rumford in Esex Bat and Marey PEARS of Ilford Spr
15.	11. John COLLINGS of Shoreditch Bat and Rebecah SHIPTON Spr
16.	11. Walter FOX of Graves End Kent Bat and Mary HAWKINS Spinster
17.	11. Richard ADAMS Batchler and Margrett REYNOLDSON
18.	12. Nicholas HALL Watchmaker and Dorothy WILLIAMS B & Spr

Folio 2 verso
19.	December 12 1678. Joseph HARPER of St Brids Batr and Eliz BOWYER Spinster
20.	13. Samuell HIGGS of Shoreditch Batr and Penelope ROBINSON Spr
21.	13. Martin BOWYER of Susex Batr and Ann RAWLINGS Widow
22.	13. James DOVE of Shew Lane Batr and Eliz ADAMS Widow
23.	14. John NICHOLS Saylor* & Batchr [and] Sarah HODGES Clarkwell** Spr
	*[*In this and similar entries, the copyist may have incorrectly written 'S' instead of 'T'. **'Clarkwell' is presumably short for Clerkenwell, Middlesex]*
24.	14. Willm JAMES of Covent Garden widr and Grace JEWELL of Do wido
25.	14. Daniel STRONG of Eling Batr and Ruth COLE Spr
26.	17. James BAKER of Kingsinton Bat and Joanna BRYAN Do Wido
27.	18. Thomas HIGGEST Marrinor Batr [and] Marey SIMPKIN Spr
28.	18. Richd WOOD marrinor & Batr [and] Jane ATTLEY of Stepney Spr
29.	19. Thos HEWS of Criplegate vintner and Batr and Eliz HALE Spr
30.	20. George EMLEY of Esex widor [and] Ann CORBETT of Ditto Spr
31.	20. Francis DAWSON Waterman Batr and Cathrine HART Spr

Folio 3 recto
32.	December 21st 1678. Lawrence SYMONDS Taylor Batr and Margt WOOD Spr
33.	24th. Ralph JENKINS of St Andrews Vintner and Batr and Alce JOHNSON Spinster
34.	26. Henry TREDWELL of Kingsington Bat and Eliz LOYSTOM Spr
35.	28. John HOBSON of Edmonton widwr and Grace HAZZARD widow
36.	29. Richd SCROOBY Jewler and Batr [and] Ann BELDUM Spinster
37.	January 2d 1678. John HOADLEY of pancrass widr and Sharlet BILLING Spr
38.	3. Richard GARDNER of St Dunstans Bat and Sarah SHAW of Do Spr
39.	5. Nicholas HILL of Lynn* Batr and Eliz TAYLOR Spr
	[*Probably King's Lynn in Norfolk]
40.	6. Richard TRUBY of Iver* Batr and Ruth HARRISON Spr
	[*Probably Iver in Buckinghamshire]
41.	7. Joshua WESTOBEY Butcher & Batr and Eliz CROSBY widow
42.	12. Nathaniel PRATT of St James Bat and Hanah CROUCH Spr
43.	13. Thos CORBETT of St Anns Soho Batr and Grace ALLEN Spr
44.	19. William MORRIS SOUTHWELL* Batr [and] Mary RAWLINGSON Spr
	[* It is possible that MORRIS is the groom's surname and SOUTHWELL his place
	of residence, but because of the uncertainty both are included in the index to
	surnames]

Folio 3 verso
45.	January 20th 1678. Thomas ROBINSON Victular Batr and Eliz CURTIS Spr
46.	21. Thomas CROSBEY of Clarkwell* Bat and Ann SYMBLE Widow
	[*'Clarkwell' is presumably short for Clerkenwell, Middlesex]
47.	22. Nickolas RATLIFE of Devis wichsr* and Jane WHITE Bat & wido
	[*Probably Wiltshire]
48.	24. Richard SHEVERS of Southwork Bat and Letis PLACE of Do Spr
49.	25th. Marmaduke HARRISON Sailmaker and Doroty COLE Batr & wido
50.	27. Charles LEWIS of St Dunstans Bat and Marey LAWRENCE Spr
51.	28. Crisr. MONGOMERY Carpr Widr and Catharine CLARKE Wido
52.	29. John JOHNSON Gardner Batr and Rebeckah HEWS Spr
53.	Feb 1st. Thomas NICHOLSON Creed Lane Batr and Eliz ELING of Do Spinster
54.	3. Leonard DALTON Marriner widr and Eliz CASEY Spr
55.	4. Charles WHITLOCK vintner Batr and Patience HARBUTT Spr
56.	6. Robt BUTTERFIELD of St Georges Bat and Martha LONGBOTTOM wido
57.	7. Nicholas FREERTON Jewrey* Batr and Emm MOORE Spr
	[*Probably St Lawrence Jewry, or Old Jewry in the City of London]

Folio 4 recto
58.	Febry 9th 1678. Jeremiah MARSHALL of Southwork B and Ruth GRIFFIN Spr
59.	12. Gibbert* DOBSON of Shoreditch Bat and Martha WISDON Spr
	[*Possibly Gilbert]
60.	16. Joseph FOOT porter Batr and Eliz GROOME widow
61.	18. John JACKSON of St Barthow* Bat and Cath RICHARDS Spr
	[*Probably St Bartholomews]
62.	24. Thos PROCTER Weaver and Batr and Elinor BROWN Spr
63.	28. Richd WARE of St Giles Taylor Bat and Rose SHAW Spinster
64.	March 2d 1678/9. Richard STEELE watchmaker & Batr
	[and] Isabella MOUNTAGUE of St Andr*, Spr
	[*Probably St Andrews Holborn]
65.	4. Joseph ELMER Marrinor Batr and Marey MASON Spr

66.   5. John CANT of St Giles Feelds widr and Eliz SEATON* Widow
      [*Possibly SEXTON]
67.   7. Nehemiah FOSTER of Bedford Batr and Ann FREEMAN Wido
68.   8. Joshua FROST of St Sepulkers Batr and Jane EAST of Do Spr
69.   11. Ezekiel RUSSELL Weavor Bat and Marey DOWGLAS Wido
70.   20. Crisr MILLS Hatter & Batr and Joahana SHORT Spr

Folio 4 verso
71.   March 25th 1679. Thos UTHWAIT of Endfield Batr and Marey FRANKLIN wdo
72.   27. Obadiah TWIST Butcher & Bat [and] Rebecah OSWALD Spr
73.   28. Mathias BANKS of St andrews* Br and Eliz WATSON Widow
      [*Probably St Andrews Holborn]
74.   29. Ambros JONES of Deptford Coopr Bat and Eleanor KING Spr
75.   30. Gillbert WATTSON Vintner Br [and] Martha TRUSO Spr
76.   30. Robt GILES of St Sepulchers Bat and Jane GREYSTON Spr
77.   April 1st 1679. Florance* DUSON Cordwiner Bat and Sarah HOOPER Spr
      [*A mistake or truly the name of the groom?]
78.   2. Anthoney HUMPHREYS Baker Bat and Susanah SIMPSON Spr
79.   3. William FOSTER Felmongr Batr [and] Sarah ALDRIGE Spr
80.   5. John EATON Hatter and Batr [and] Marey TRUBY Widow
81.   6. Richard FRAWHOCK Pinmaker Bat and Alce REYNOLDS Spr
82.   7. Richard CROWLEY Gent Servt Bat and Jane REEVES Spr

Folio 5 recto
83.   April 10th 1679. Thos REYNOLDS Brewer widr and Catrn FELOWS wido
84.   11. James Vinsent LAMBERT* Batr and Jane LANE Widow
      [*It is possible that this entry has been incorrectly copied from an entry for James
      VINSENT, or VINCENT, of Lambeth]
85.   12. John DEAN of Blackfryers Batr and Martha FIELD Spr
86.   13. Jos CHURCH weavor & Batr [and] Alce FENLEY Spr
87.   13. Willm GOY* of St Brids Widow and Jenia WILKINS Widow
      [*Possibly GAY]
88.   15. Robt WHITEHEAD and Ann FOSTIN Batr & Spr
89.   17. Eliz* WEBB of St Clemants Dans Bat and Marey FOSTER Spr
      [*This appears to be a mistake, perhaps an error for 'Edw']
90.   18. Jonathan WARD Carman Batr and Martha ENGROVE wido
91.   19. Edward SAMPLE of purple Lane widr [and] Sarah WATTSON Widow
92.   21. Richard RIGHT Butcher widr and Avis JUXTON wido
93.   22. William BUCKLAND weavor Batr and Cath. COTTELL Spr
94.   23. Henry GREEN Sadler & Batr [and] Jane GREEN of Do Spr

Folio 5 verso
95.   April 23d 1679. John the son of Joseph & Eliz HARCOTT was Baptz.
96.   25. Robert STOWELL of St James widr [and] Martha FREEMAN Widow
97.   25. Gregory SMALLBONES Butcher and Jane GUEST Bat & wido
98.   29. Crisr. PEARPOINT of St Marys Bat [and] Maria BLAKE widow
99.   30. William WATTSON Braysier Br and Eliz FROLICK Spr
100. 30. James POWELL Marriner Batr and Marey JENKINS Spr
101. May 1st 1679. Jere. TAPPING Perfumer Widr and Sarah MASTERS Spr
102. 2d. Ezekill DEANNE Westr* Batr and Ann CLACK Spr
      [* Probably short for Westminster]

103.	5. Richard CRAWLEY Watchmaker Bt and Elinor DAY Widow
104.	6. James STEWARD Taylor Batr and Jane PORTER Widow
105.	7. William HONDER Scoolmaster Br and Eliz UNDERWOOD Spr

Folio 6 recto

106.	May 7th 1679 Baptized Wm the son of William & Marry MORRIS of Robins wood Court Shoe Lane
107.	9. Gabrell FULLER of St Albons* Batr and Marey HURTON Spr
	[*Probably St Albans in Hertfordshire, but possibly St Alban, Wood Street in the City of London]
108.	10. Edmond JEWELL of wt Chapell Br and Isabella MAY Spr
109.	11. Nehemiah SHORT Batr and Isabella LIONS Spr
110.	11. Alexr BALLS of Ross Herefordsr & B and Marey GIBBS of Do Spr
111.	12. Mark MORRIS Farmer Widr and WHITE Grace Widow
112.	12. William SHARD Barber Batr and Constance FIRTH Wido
113.	12. Nehema. SADLER Victler Batr and Jane MITCHELL Widow
114.	13. Richard POWELL Carpenter Batr and Francis DUDLEY Wido
115.	14. John JACKSON Taylor Batr and Eliz CARTER Spr
116.	15. Gabl. RIGHT of Cheshire widr and Kezia BROWN Spr

Folio 6 verso

117.	May 18th 1679. Richard HAINES Batr and Reba. HOWARD Spr
118.	19. Ralph PHILLIPS Marrinor Bat and Grace ROBERTS Spr
119.	22. Richard OSWYN Sidler* Widr and Henrietta GREEN wido
	[*Probably sadler]
120.	23. Mathew THOMSON Waterman Br and Marey FROST Spr
121.	24. James WATERS Silversmith Bat and Cathn. REYNOLDS Spr
122.	25. John DORRINGTON Taylor Batr and Penelope WILMOT wido
123.	26. John HARPER weavor Batr and Eliz BOSWELL Spr
124.	28. James SHIPPEY Waterman W and Letitia MORRIS wido
125.	30. Crisr DURANTT weaver Bat and Eliz LUIS Spr
126.	30. James THOMSON Gardner Bat and Hester COOKE Spr
127.	30. Leonard WIGGIN Batr and Catn. WYATT Spr

Folio 7 recto

128.	June 4th 1679. John SPENCER of Iver* Batr and Eliz URLIN Spr
	[*Probably Iver in Buckinghamshire]
129.	6. Richard RUSSELL Tanner [and] Marey JONES Bat & Spr
130.	19. Abram. HARRINGTON Bat and Jane WILLSON Spr
131.	20. Daniel GOLBY Porter Batr and Ann JOHNSON Spr
132.	21. Wm PRITCHARD Winsor* Batr and Marey BOLTON Spr
	[*Probably Windsor in Berkshire]
133.	29. Richard STEVENS Horsler Bat and Jane WATKINS Spr
134.	29. Wm SAMPLE Carpr Batr and Marey BLAKE wido
135.	30. John DICKSON Butcher Bat and Eliz GOODALL Spr
136.	July 1st. Thomas NEVILL Soho Widr and Faith EDWARDS Spr
137.	2. Thos BARNES Furier Batr [and] Dorcas GRAVES Spr

Folio 7 verso

| 138. | July 3d 1679. Gregory MILLS Kent Bat and Marey CLARK Spr |

139.　5. Mordecai CROSSLEY Button Bat and Jane BROOM Spr
140.　10. John GROOM Collermaker Bat and Ann PLASTEED Wido
141.　12. Jeremiah LAWE Corkman Bat and Christian MILLS Spr
142.　14. John JONES of Denbigh Batr and Barbara PEIRCE Wido
143.　15. George GORE Tring in Hartsr. Bat and Marey COLLINS Spr
144.　20. Ferdinando KEAT Butcher & B and Marria SWIFT Spr
145.　23. Edmond KINGTON of Norf* Batr and Judith MARRIOTT wido
　　　　*[*Probably short for Norfolk]*
146.　25. George BECKET Cordwiner Bat and Susanah BOWS Wido
147.　August 4th 1679. Robt HILL Taylor Batr and Ann WARNE Spr
　　　　*[The groom's name (but not the bride's) is repeated in entry 352, but that entry is
　　　　dated 14 May 1706/7]*
148.　5. William FALKNER Bat and Eliz HILL Spr
　　　　*[This entry is repeated at entry 353, but dated 14 May 1706/7, and the groom's
　　　　surname is spelt differently]*

Folio 8 recto
149.　Augt 7th 1679. Edward RICHARD Sadler Batr and Marey UNDERWOOD wido
　　　　*[This entry is repeated at entry 354, but dated 15 May 1706/7, and the groom's
　　　　surname is spelt differently]*
150.　12. Joseph PHILLIPS Labr Bat and Joahana FALKNER Spr
　　　　*[A groom of this name, but a widower, also appears in entry 355, which is dated
　　　　16 May 1706/7]*
151.　19. Marmaduke LATCHMAN Batr and Eliz BROWN Spr
152.　21. Charles BROWN Waterman Bat and Agnes GARDINER Spr
153.　28. Henry SNELLING Jack smith Bat and Francis GREEN Spr
154.　September 1st. Thos REDFARN St Ands Batr and Margt WILLIAMS wido
　　　　*[This entry is repeated at entry 356, but dated 17 May 1706/7, and the groom's
　　　　surname is spelt differently with his status (Gent) noted instead of his residence
　　　　(St Ands, or St Andrews)]*
155.　2. Baptzed Wm FREEMAN a Black belonging to Captn ETHERIDGE in Pickdilley
　　　　*[This entry is repeated at entry 357, but dated 17 May 1706/7, and the captain's
　　　　surname is spelt differently]*
156.　3. Edward CLAYTON Batr and Eliz RICHARDSON Sp
157.　4. George FENNER Cordwiner & Sarah BENNETT Widow

Folio 8 verso
158.　September 5th 1679. Crisr FRANKLIN Batr and Marey FOX Spr
159.　5. James NEWBURY Distiller Bat and Susana VEAL Spr
160.　7. Thos TATLOCK of St Giles Bat and Eliz JOHNSON Spr
　　　　*[This entry is repeated at entry 358, but dated 18 May 1706/7, and the groom's
　　　　occupation (cordwainer) is noted instead of his residence (St Giles)]*
161.　7. Charles BARLAND Tapster Bat and Elinor LOCK Spr
162.　9. Peatir TAYLOR Carman Batr and Ann TURNER Spr
163.　11. William ARIS Labr Batr and Marey HITCHCOCK
164.　12. Daniel EVANS Bromley* Bat and Margrett CRAWLEY wido
　　　　*[*In Kent]*
165.　14. John JACKEMAN Fellmonger [and] Isabella HEWIT B & Spr
166.　15. Patrick DASHWOOD Butcher and Penope ALLCOCK Spr

167.	18. Aron STEWARD Smith Batr and Sarah SLY Spr

167. 18. Aron STEWARD Smith Batr and Sarah SLY Spr
[This entry is repeated at entry 359, but dated 19 May 1706/7, and the groom's surname is noted as SHEPARD instead of STEWARD, his occupation as a mariner instead of a smith]

168. 19. Mathew HEWIT Aldgate Batr [and] Agnes MERRIAM Spr

Folio 9 recto

169. Sept 20th 1679. Christopher COTTRELL Fishman B and Marey PRICE wido

170. 21. Nicholas SEATON Farmer Bat and Eliz MANBY Spr

171. 23. Charles KEAVES weavor Bat and Ruth SINGCLEAR* Wido
*[*Probably an incorrect spelling of SINCLAIR]*

172. 24. Charles BROWN Gent of Finchley Bat and Bennet GARDENER Spr
[It appears that this entry has been written over an area where another entry had been rubbed out]

173. 28. Thomas LETHAHIR Gent & Batr and Henrieta Maria Dorotha JENINGS Spr St Martins Lane

174. October 2d. Gregory FULLER Crook Lane B and Eliz ALLFORD widow

175. 5. Ralph NORRIS Bookseller Bat [and] Jane NAYLOR Widow

176. 6. Andrew SMITH Painter widr and Sarah FRANKLIN wido

177. 7. Allen BRADLEY marinor Batr and Hanah GIBBSON Spr

178. 8. Danel CRAY Porter Batr [and] Hanah* Marey AUSTIN Spr
['Hanah' has been crossed out. Note that Hannah is the name of the bride in the previous entry, which suggests that the clerk is copying these entries from another source]*

Folio 9 verso

179. October 9th 1679. George TRIBE Batr [and] Elin DILLEW Spr

180. 10. Charles KENT Stone Cutter Bat and Susanah PEIRCE Spr

181. 12. William BROOKS Batr and Jane STEARS Spr

182. 19. Thos BOWLER Spectlemaker Bat and Marey OSBORN Sp

183. January 9th 1706. Hen WINCH marrinor Batr and Eliz BOWLES Spr
[Despite the jump of 26 years between between this and the last entry, the same handwriting continues]

184. 9. Thos BILL marrinor Batr and Reba* GREENWAY Spr
*[*Short for Rebecca]*

185. 9. Thos BURTON Husbd.man widr and Eliz EVINS Spr
[The bride's name is the same in this and the following entry, suggesting a mistake by the person copying from the original entries]

186. 9. James HUMMERSTONE Gardn. Bat and Eliz EVINS Spr
[The bride's name is the same in this and the previous entry, suggesting a mistake by the person copying from the original entries]

187. 10. Anthoney BLOSS Marr and Bat & Margrett HOWARD spr both of St Anns Limehouse

188. 10. John GUSTON Soulder Batr [and] Mary DAVIS Wido

Folio 10 recto

189. January 11th 1706. Samuell WILLIAMS Cooper Bat and Ann RAWLINGS wido

190. 12. Mickel DOYLE Gent Batr and Fras. FANNING Wido

191. 13. Thos MARSHALL Saylor* Batr and Ann TALBOTT Spr
*[*The copyist may have incorrectly written 'S' instead of 'T']*

192. 13. John HUBBARD Taylor Batr and Elinor HARRIS Spr

193.   13. John WRIGHT Marrinor Batr and Ann PHRASIER* Spr
        [*Presumably FRASIER]
194.   13. John KENT Labr Widowr and Frans. HIGGS Wido
195.   14. Edward CLARE Labr Widwr and Catn. NICHOL Spr
196.   14. Willm JONES Marrinor widwr and Reba MALLERY Wido
197.   15. John MANNING Marrinor Bat and Magln* WILLIAMS Spr
        [*Probably short for Magdalen]
198.   Richard MAN Marrinor Bat and Marey YARDLEY Spr
        [This entry is undated but the layout of the page suggests that it was entered as a
        marriage of the same date as entry 197]
199.   16. Thos GLADWIN Cordwiner Batr and Marey HART Spr

Folio 10 verso
200.   Januarey 18th 1706. Richard HAYNES Butcher Bat and Ann FOSTER Spr
201.   19. Joseph GUILFORD Saylor* Bat and Ann STEED Spr
        [*The copyist may have incorrectly written 'S' instead of 'T']
202.   19. John PROSSER victler Batr [and] Marey FISHER Spr
203.   20. Andrew BRAIN Sailor Bat and Elinor WATSON Spr
204.   21. Henry BURTON Marrinor Bat and Philadelphia STANLEY wido
205.   23. George MISHARD weavor Bat and Hannah GREGORY Sp
206.   24. Will HEATHTHORNE porter Batr and Catn THIRFT* wido
        [*Possibly THIRST]
207.   29. John FELING Saylor* Batr and Ann SIMMS Spr
        [*The copyist may have incorrectly written 'S' instead of 'T']
208.   29. John WHITE marrinor Bat and Ann GILL Spr
209.   29. Thos MASEY Soulder Widowr and Grace HILL wido

Folio 11 recto
210.   Feb 1st 1706. Francis PELL Soulder widwr and Margret CLIFTON wido
211.   1st. Thos AVERLIN Baker widr and Eliz BAYLEY Spr
212.   2. Robt JONES Marrinor Bat and Deborah TURBEL Spr
213.   2. Francis FISH marrinor B [and] Eliz WHITEHEAD Spr
214.   2. John TRUDGION Saylor* Batr and Jane MULLET Spr
        [*The copyist may have incorrectly written 'S' instead of 'T']
215.   2. Thos HOBBS Carman Batr and Izabela DOD wido
216.   2. Robt MOORE Lanr Batr and Ann COURTEE Wido
217.   2. Jonath. PEARCE Coachman Bat and Charity EADY Spr
218.   2. Thos PANTON Brewer Batr and Sarah CHIPPERTON Sp
219.   3. John SMITH Taylor Bat and Alce WALL Spr

Folio 11 verso
220.   Feb 3d 1706. John CUBBIDGE Taylor Batr and Mary LEONARD Spr
221.   3. John HUTCHINSON Taylor widr and Alce JONES widow
222.   4. William SOMMERS Porter widr and Eliz WICKS widow
223.   4. John ROSS Chelsa* Widowr and Eustice WARWICK wido
        [*Presumably Chelsea]
224.   4. John MOORE Marrinor Bat and Marey WEBBSTER Spr
225.   5. Robt HALL Cooper Batcheldr and Marey BALL Spr
226.   5. Jacob PRICE Carpenter Widr and Jane SOUTHERN Wido
227.   5. John WILLIAMS Taylor Widr and Bridgett FOSTER Wido

228.   6. Edward PHIPPS Waterman Batr and Jane GRATEY Wido
         [This entry is repeated at entry 346, but dated 2 May 1706/7, and the bride's surname appears as GRACE]
229.   6. Francis CARTER Vintner Batr and Marey JURDON Spr
230.   6. Thos PITTS of Ditton Batr and Eliz COOK Spr
         [This entry is repeated at entry 347, but dated 4 May 1706/7]

Folio 12 recto
231.   Feb 6th 1706. John HUGGINS of Iver* Bat and Ann LANGLEY Spr
         *[*Probably Iver in Buckinghamshire. This entry is repeated at entry 344, but dated 30 April 1706/7, and the bride's surname appears as CANSLEY]*
232.   6. Richard ELLIS Coopr Batr and Marey PROCTER Sp
233.   6. John BARWOOD Marinor Bat and Barth DANISON Spr
234.   8. James HUME Hatter Batr and Sarah BROWN Spr
235.   8. George WATTSON Cordwiner Bat and Susan SCARFE wido
236.   9. Henry PLATT Smith Batr and Marey PURSON wido
237.   9. John SMITH of Aldgate Batr and Ann GUNSTON Wido
238.   9. William MALLARD Butcher and Maria WHARFF Wido
239.   9. Erasmus LAWSON Batchler and Catn PLATT Widow
240.   9. Edward CASTEEN Cordwiner Bat and Marey EVINS Wido
241.   9. Danel. CHARELLEIRETT Batr and Eliz SAVAGE Spr

Folio 12 verso
242.   Feb ye 9th 1706. William GILBERT Cordwiner B and Eliz KNIGHT wido
243.   9. John YOUNG Marrinor Bat and Ann GREEN Spr
244.   10. Richard SMITH Marrinor Bat and Martha GREEN Spr
245.   10. James MORTON Gent Servt Batr and Margret BONIBRIDGE of Watling st Spr
246.   10. Richd MARTIN Vintner Bat and Eliz BRUSH Spr
247.   10. John RICHES Marrinor Bat and Eliz WALKER Spr
248.   11. Richard HUTCHINSON Batr and Eliz LUCAS Wido
249.   11. Joseph MAYHEW Leatherd* widr and Sarah BATES Spr
         *[*Short for leatherdresser]*
250.   12. Auther* BERRY Husbdman Batr and Marey WOOD Spr
         *[*Probably a mistake for Arthur]*
251.   13. Robt RICHARDS Cordwiner Bat and Rebeca BLACKMORE Spr

Folio 13 recto
252.   Feb 13th 1706. Richd PINSIN Blacksmith B and Jane CLARK widow
253.   13. John DAVIS Marrinor & wido and Marey STAPLE Spr
254.   14. Will SWAIN Soulder & Batr and Eliz DENNIS wido
255.   14. David DOLLEY Marinor Bat and Eliz RODGERS wido
256.   14. Phillip GARDNER waterman wdr and Sarah EVINS wido
257.   15. Emanuel SOZER Marrinor Bat and Ann READ Deptford Spr
258.   15. Rice PRICHARD Marrinor Bat and Magdalin DAVIS Spr
259.   15. Thos MITCHELL Marinor widr and Judeth BLUNDEN Spr
260.   15. Francis WRIGHT Carpenter wido and Martha WILKINSON Sp
261.   16. John GUFFECK Plaistrer Bat and Hannah KEEN Spr

Folio 13 verso

262. Feb 16th 1706. John TAYLOR feltmaker Bat and Dorcas HULL* widow
      *[*Possibly HALL]*
263. 17. John GOODMAN Labr Widr and Marey LOCKEY wido
264. 18. John PALMER Bricklayer Bat and Eliz COATS Spr
265. 18. John ROBINSON Gent Servt Bat and *PHIPSON Spr
      *[*The bride's Christian name is not recorded]*
266. 18. Evan OWENS Victler widwr and Jone MORGAN Spr
267. 18. Willm PLAW Gardner Bat and Eliz TAYLOR wido
268. 19. John WHERLOW Gardner Bat and Marey FIELD Spr
269. 19. John NORWAY Taylor widr and Ann PEEKE Spr
270. 20. John SMITH frame maker and Jane HARPER Sp & B*
      *[*Presumably an error for 'B & Sp']*
271. 20. Andrew BROOME vintner & Bat and Martha WATERS Spr

Folio 14 recto

272. Feb 21st 1706. William SHUTER Taylor & Bat and Marey SONGHURST Spr
273. 21. Nathaniel RODGERS Batr and Hanah CORNINGHAM*
      *[*Possibly COMINGHAM. The bride's condition is not stated]*
274. 22. Will GORRING Butcher Bat [and] Martha HALL Spr
275. 22. Jos SIMPSON porter widr and Margrett DUNBAR wido
276. 22. John KELLEY marrinor Batr and Eliz AUSTIN Spr
277. 23. John EDWARDS Soulder Batr and Grace CHILD Spr
278. 23. John SWEET Joyner Batr and Edeth HOW Spr
279. 23. Thos WHITRELL Cordwiner Bat and Marey COLE Spr
280. 25. Peater MOCHLORD waterman B and Marey MINGO Spr
281. 25. Robt COLEY Saylor* Batr [and] Marey VESEY widow
      *[*The copyist may have incorrectly written 'S' instead of 'T']*
282. 25. Richard DICKERSON widor and Eliz TOWNSEND Spr

Folio 14 verso

283. Feb 25th 1706. Arthor COOPER Labr Widr and Eliz LUKE wido
284. 25. Bartholomew BENNET Carter B and Eliz STEVENS Spr
285. 25. Sam NIXON Labr and Bat and Marth HORNWELL Spr
286. 26. Peater Julian BRINKINFE Bat and Marey FRANCISCO Spr
287. 27. George GREEN Brickmaker Bat and Marey SOWDEN wido
288. 27. Charles CARRAWAY Saylor* Batr and Marey NISLER wido
      *[*The copyist may have incorrectly written 'S' instead of 'T']*
289. March 1st 1706. Thos HAMOND Lighterman Bat and Eliz TOMPSON Spr
290. 2. Abraham BALDWIN Widowr and RIDGMENT Marey* Wido
      *[*The bride's surname appears before her Christian name]*
291. 2. William CARTER Vintner Batr and Ann ADAMS Spr
292. 2. James HIRST Sugar Baker Bat and Grace BOTTHAMLY Sp

Folio 15 recto

293. March 3rd 1706. John FIGGERS Chapman Batr and Martha MOYNARD wido
294. 3. Richd STAFFORD Soulder Batr and Ann BENNETT widow
295. 4. Joseph KNIGHT Labr Batr and Dorothy LOXLEY spr
296. 11. Walter CISIL* Gent Batr and Lucy GREENLEAF Spr
      *[*Probably an error for CECIL]*

297.   12. Edward WOOD of Kent Batr and Eliz CHATHLEY* wido
        [*Possibly CHALKLEY]
298.   12. Humphrey LANE Souldr Bat and Joyce ARIS Widow
299.   13. Wm DAVIS Victuler & Batr and Patience HIDE Spr
300.   13. Sam GOSNELL Saylor* & Batr and Marey CRUMER wido
        [*The copyist may have incorrectly written 'S' instead of 'T']
301.   14. William HORTON Drumer Batr and Eliz GRYNES Spr
302.   15. John FLETCHER Brewer Bat and Debroah EAMS Spr
303.   15. John ANDO Black man Batr and Joanah CHESTER Black Woman Spr

Folio 15 verso
304.   March 16th 1706. Richd HOULDING mariner Bat and Marey VOPALTER wido
305.   16. Richard HULL Taylor & Batr and Eliz BRIGGS wido
306.   16. Edward HOWARD Cordwiner Widow and Margrett PAIN Wido
307.   17. Richd DAVIS Culenden & Bat and Marey DAVIS wido
308.   17. John BARLEY marinor Bat and Ann MALLASH spr
309.   17. William GORE Cordwiner widr and Ctrine* EVANES Spr
        [*Short for Catherine]
310.   18. Charles BENNETT Carpenter Bat and Sarah MAIDEN Spr
311.   18. George DARLING marinor Batr and Margrett ALLEN Spr
312.   19. Thomas LEWGAR Surgon & widow and BRAND Marey* Spr
        [*The bride's surname appears before her Christian name]
313.   19. William DAVIS Clothworker & Bat and Marey IMBER Spr
314.   20. Robt WRIGHT Saylor* widowr and Ann MORGAN wido
        [*The copyist may have incorrectly written 'S' instead of 'T']

Folio 16 recto
315.   March 20th 1706. John MARTIN Turner Batr and Rebea* BRASIER Spr
        [*Short for Rebecca]
316.   20. Andrew MUSCOREY Sailor Batr and Eliz NAILES Spr
317.   21. Samuell SIMPSON Marinor Bat and Marey HAYES widow
318.   22. Lawrence SHEPPARD of Chesee* Batr and Martha DUNSTAN Spr
        [*Probably Chelsea]
319.   23. Thomas LOW Cordwiner and Batr and Eliz ALDEN Widor
320.   23. Mark M DE HONE* weavor Batr and Joanah BALLARD Spr
        [*There are two gaps in this name, as indicated]
321.   24. Charles MASON Labr and Batr and Ann MAZE widow
322.   24. Thos GRAY Jockey and Batr and Lydia KETCHMY Spr
323.   24. John DALE Marrinor & Batr and Ann ELDRIDGE Spr
324.   24. John HALDEN Coachman widr and Marey STEVENS wido
325.   24. William STEPHENSON Taylor Bat and Sarah DAWSON Spr

Folio 16 verso
326.   March 24th 1706/7. Antoney ALVERADO Gent Bat and Marey RODGERS Spr
327.   25. Ingebright LAWRENSON Bat and Eliz ANDERSON Wido
328.   25. John ALISON Clarkwell* widr and Ann GREENAWAY Spr
        [*'Clarkwell' is presumably short for Clerkenwell, Middlesex]
329.   26. William NOCK St Martins Widr and Marey CLEAVER wido
330.   27. Edward PENN Vintner Bat and Susanah BATTEY Spr
331.   27. John SAWYER Barber Batr and Marey SHORT wido

332.	28. John BEALE Gardner Batr and Ann GINN Spr
333.	29. Thos HOLTON Waterman Bat and Marey EDWARDS Spr
334.	29. Alexander CARNEY Widwr and Eliz SANER* Wido
	[*The last two letters of this name are unclear, and unlike the usual hand of the writer]
335.	29. Timoy* YOUNG Cooper Batr and Marey WILSON Spr
	[*Probably a short form for Timothy]

Folio 17 recto

336.	April 2d 1706/7 Thos WALHER* Cordwiner Bat and Marey JENKINS Spr
	[*Possibly WALKER]
337.	4. Will SOYER Butcher widr and Marey GREEN Wido
338.	10. Will JONES Plaisr* Batr and Jane SMART Spr
	[*Probably short for Plaisterer]
339.	16. John TEMPLE of St Katharines Batr & Vintner & Mary CRACKWELL Spr
	[This entry has been written over an area from which it appears that another entry has been erased]
340.	18. Wm BRODIX Gent Batr and Ann BROWNING Spr
341.	18. Edward MUNDAY St Anns Bat and Marey MOORE Spr
342.	25. Thos MILLS Weaver Batr and Marey MARGIN Spr
343.	29. Richd MARTIN Vintner Bat and Eliz PITTS Spr
344.	30. John HUGGINS of Iver* Bat and Ann CANSLEY Spr
	[*Probably Iver in Buckinghamshire. This entry repeats entry 231, except that the bride's surname appears as LANGLEY and it has a different date]
345.	30. Geo: GREEN Uxbridg Batr and Jane LOVE Do Spr

Folio 17 verso

346.	May 2d 1706/7. Edward PHIPPS waterman Bat and Jane GRACE Spr
	[This entry repeats entry 228, except that the bride's surname appears as GRATEY and it has a different date]
347.	4. Thos PITTS of Ditton Batr and Eliz COOK Spr
	[This entry repeats entry 230 but with a different date]
348.	10. William MITCHELL Spr & B and Marey MOORE
349.	11. Danll CRAY Porter and Bat and Marey DILLEN Spr
350.	11. Robt RAGG of St Sepukers Bat and Catn. BRELEIBON Spr
351.	12. Charles TOLETT Widowr B* and Marey MONK Spr
	[*The description of this groom as both a widower and as B, or bachelor, is probably a copying error. It is likely that he was a bachelor and that 'Widowr' has been incorrectly copied from the groom's occupation]
352.	14. Robt HILL Taylor Batr and Ann TURNER Spr
	[The groom's name (but not the bride's name) is repeated from entry 147, which also has a different date]
353.	14. Will FOLKNER Perukmaker Bat and Eliz HILL Spr
	[This entry repeats entry 148 but with a different date and a different spelling of the groom's surname]
354.	15. Edward RICHARDS Sadler Bat and Marey UNDERWOOD Spr
	[This entry repeats entry 149 but with a different date and a different spelling of the groom's surname]
355.	16. Joseph PHILLIPS Widowr and Jane BROOKS Spr
	[The groom's name (but not the bride's name) also appears at entry 150, but with a different date]

Folio 18 recto
356. May 16th 1706/7. Thos REDFRAME Gent Batr and Margt WILLIAMS Spr
[This entry repeats entry 154 but with a different date, the groom's surname is spelt differently and the groom's status (Gent) is noted instead of his residence (St Ands, or St Andrews)]
357. 17. Baptizd. Wm FREEMAN a Black belonging to Capt ELDRIDGE Pickdily
[This entry repeats entry 155 but with a different date and the captain's surname is spelt differently]
358. 18. Thos TATLOCK Cordwiner Bat and Eliz JOHNSON Spr
[This entry repeats entry 160 but with different date and the groom's occupation (cordwainer) is noted instead of his residence (St Giles)]
359. 19. Aron SHEPARD Marinor Bat and Sarah SLY Spr
[This entry repeats entry 167 but with a different date, the surname SHEPARD for the groom instead of STEWARD, and his occupation as a mariner instead of a smith]
360. 19. Mathew ELIOTT Barber & Bat and Sarah SMITH Widow
361. 20. William WHITE Batchler and Eliz GOODALL Spr
362. 22. Tobias LANE Batr and Marey SMITH Spr
363. 25. John BODALL of St Clemants Batr & Margret VIRENT Spr
364. 26. John FRESHWATER Batr and Ann STACEY Spr

Folio 18 verso
365. August 8th 1706/7 John YOUNG and Elizth DANIEL Sanhope
366. January 28th 1706/7 Wm PYNSENT als PINSON of Stansted* Surgon & Widr and Elizth BROWN of the same Wido
*[*In Essex]*
367. August 4th 1707 Wm EDWARD Gent Servt of Chealsea Batch and Frances DELANY of St Brides Spinsr. Cuthbert
368. April 8 1708. Saml FEAR and Elizth HOGGINS we* married at the Golden Ball in the Old Baily. p. Pretty
*[*Short for 'were']*
369. Feby 5th 1708. Edmd TAYLOR Apothecary Covt Garden B and Susanna MARKS of Do Spr Jones
370. Feby 6 1708. John DERRICK of St Olives Hart Street Batch & Mary HANNAN of Ditto Mottram
371. 6. Wm HALL of Bishgate street Frame work knitter and Batchr & Mary WEBB of Do. Spinr. Mottram
372. 6. John STEPHENS of Aldgate Boxmakr & Bat and Elizth KINGHAM of St Johns Wapping Mottram
373. 7th. Thomas WRIGHT of Aldgate Batch and Elizth HULL of Do Spr p Mottram

Folio 19 recto
374. March 2 1709. 2. Luke REDMAN of fulham Cooper and Ann POULTON Do Br spr p Mottram
375. 2. Thos KEETH of St Mary White Chapel & Elizth PLUMMER Do W. W
376. 3. George ROTLEDGE of Ratliff Sawyer & Mary ESTON Do Br. Spr.
377. 4. Willm PLATTS St Bennetts pauls Warf Chairmaker & Sarah WALKER Do Br. Spr
378. * Jeremiah DWYER of St Catherns Coleman Gent Sernt & Mary JOHNSON Do W. Spr
[This entry is undated but the layout of the page suggests that it was entered as a marriage of the same date as entry 377]

379.   5. Fran: THOMAS of St James Westmr & Ann WEBBER Do Br W
380.   5. Giles FREMAN of Pettersham Husbandn.
       & Elizth GALLINGTON of Richmond* W W
       [* In Surrey]
381.   6. Richd BIDDELL St Martins ye fields Gent Coachman
       & Mary BARNES of St Andrews Holbourn Br W

Folio 19 verso
382.   April 1709. 17. John VEREY of Coleman Street Corwn*
       & Abigal SANDERS of Clare Street B Spr p Mottram
       [*Probably a cordwainer]
383.   18. John BIBBY Br & Gentn. Sernt of St Jameses Sqr
       & Jane COLGROVE Do Spr p Mottram
384.   18. Robert ANDREWS of Mile End new Town Rope maker
       & Ann GAMES Do Br Spr p Mottram
385.   20. George CARUTHIS of Uxbridge Middx Meelman & Mary ROBERTS Br. Spr.
386.   20. John CLARKE of Battersea Collermaker & Jane BOOT Br. Spr. p Mottram
387.   22. Thos TURNER of St Anns Blackfriers Callender & Ann PLUMER Br. Spr
388.   22. John WHITE of St Martins ye fields Gardner
       & Magdalen BURRIDGE Do W W Jones

Folio 20 recto
389.   May 1709. 22. Edmond HUNT of Eaton* Surgeon
       & Susanah GRAY of Windsor W. W pr. Pretty
       [*Presumably Eton in Berkshire]
390.   23. Willm REVELL of Barking Esx Labr & Elizth BATSTONE Do Br Spr
391.   23. William JACKSON of Battersea Sailor & Mary BATEMAN Do W W. pr Pretty
392.   24. Morgan BOWEN of St Clemans Danes perukemaker
       & Margret ANISTEN Do Br. wid
393.   24. John CATEN of Hadley Kent Husbandn
       & Mary HALL of Seals Kent Br. Spr. pr Mottram
394.   25. Jams. COCKRAM of Stepney weaver Br & Mary SMITH Do Spr pr Pretty
395.   *Thos DAVIS of fulham Green & Ann ASHWOOD Do Br. Spr. Jones
       [This entry is undated but the layout of the page suggests that it was entered as a
       marriage of the same date as entry 394]

Folio 20 verso
396.   July 1709. 4. William PATTEN of St Giles ye fields Sailor
       & Elizth HUDSON of St Mary White Chapel B. W. Jones
397.   10. Thos PEERS of Durham Marn. & Frances FENNICK Do Br. Spr.
398.   10. Andrew PETTERSON of Greenwich Appothecary
       & Mary MOORE Do Br Spr Pretty
399.   19. Willm RENNOLLS of St Brides watchmaker & Sarah TURNER Br. Spr
400.   Henry TROTTER 1st Regnt Guards Soilder & Mary PRATT St James westmr B. W
       [This entry is undated but the layout of the page suggests that it was entered as a
       marriage of the same date as entry 399]
401.   20. Theodorus HARTLEY of Wapping Marr. & Elizth HARDY Do Br Spr
402.   John DALE of Kingston upon Thames Timber mernt* & Eliz COCKS Do Wr. W Pretty
       [*Probably short for merchant. This entry is undated but the layout of the page
       suggests that it was entered as a marriage of the same date as entry 401]

Folio 21 recto
403.　August 1709. 4. Thos SIMMONS of St Andrews Holbourn wheelwright
　　　 & Ann ROBERTS Do W W p Jones
404.　8. Willm BOWDEN of Twittenham Gardner & Sarah GRAVENOR Br. Spr
405.　12. Frederick SMITH of St Katherin Surgeon & Elizth ORTON Do Br. Spr. Mottram
406.　16. John CLARKE of Essex fisherman & Mary SMALL of fowles nest pr. W. W
407.　20. Edmond MARKLAND of St James Chareman
　　　 & Mary GREEN Do Br Spr Mottram
408.　22. Willm HODGES of St Dunstans Stepney Baker
　　　 & Sarah LANGVILE Br. Spr. Mottram
409.　26. Richd STUARD of Walton on Thames Gardner
　　　 & Jane MAIN of Wht. Chapel Br Spr
410.　30. James SEAGER of Warter lane Fleet street
　　　 & Jane HEWETT of St Brides Br. Spr. Jones

Folio 21 verso
411.　Septbr 1709. 5. Samuell GRAY of Shoreditch Gent
　　　 & Ann PREIST of Aldgate Wr. W. Pretty
412.　9. John COBBY of Sussx. Marr. & Mary STEEL of St Olives Southwark Br. Spr
413.　12. Joshua BOWSER of St Savors Southwk waterman & Ann HERBERT Do Br. Wr.
414.　17. Will CARE of St Martins ye fields Gent Sernt & Margret PALMER Do Br Spr
415.　20. Edward RYLANDS of St Margts westmr
　　　 & Mary REYNER of St James westmr Br Spr Jones
416.　24. John BOLTON of St Brides weaver & Ann BERRY Do Wr. Spr
417.　27. Charles LAVINGTON of Blackwall Attorneys Clerk
　　　 & Margt GOOD of Rederiff Br Spr

Folio 22 recto
418.　Septer 1709. 28. Thomas TALLCOTT of X Ch par Rasor maker
　　　 & Ann GLOVER Do Br. Spr p Mottram
419.　29. Thos POWELL of St Sepulchres Cordwn. & Margt FRICKER Do Br Spr Jones
420.　29. John KIRBY of Enfield wool Comber & Mary EADES Do Br. Spr
421.　30. Edwd WINWOOD of St Andrews Holbourn Gent & Ann SMITH Do W & W
422.　30. Benjamin SPENCER of Aldgate Tayler & Ann MILLS of Shadwell
　　　 [The spouses' conditions are not recorded]
423.　30. Benjn. ROGERS of Staines Midx & Susanah JORDAN of Hartfordshr. Wr. Spr.
424.　Richd TURNER of Salisbury* Gent & Rachel WILLIAMS Br. Sp Jones
　　　 *[*In Wiltshire. This entry is undated but the layout of the page suggests that it
　　　 was entered as a marriage of the same date as entry 423]*

Folio 22 verso
425.　Octob 1709. * Benjamen NORRIS Carpenter
　　　 and Eliz HUNT of St andrews Holborn Spinster
　　　 [*No specific date is noted]
426.　Novemb 1709. 8. Will HOULTERRICE* of St Andrews Holborn Porter
　　　 & Catharine HURSTE of Ditto Bat Widow
　　　 [*This name is very unclear]
427.　Decemer. ye 12: 1709. Thos STAFFES of Deptford Kent Bat
　　　 & Mary PARRAT of Dartford Ditto Spinster
428.　14. John CASS of St Giles ye fields Joyner & Elizth BAYLEY Br Spr

Folio 23 recto

429.   ffebey. 9th 1725. Benjamen OLIVER of St Martins Camp Servt and Batchr
and Sarah PETTIT of St James' Spinr. p Mottram
[Despite the jump of 15 years between between this and the last entry, the same handwriting continues]

430.   August 6th 1728. Francis HILL of St Dunstans in ye East Tayler & Batchr
and Dorothy POUTTNEY of Ditto Spr Floyd
[Despite the jump of three years between between this and the last entry, the same handwriting continues]

431.   6th. William HUMBLE of St Giles's Widr and Sarah ROBERTS of Do. Spr Floyd

432.   6. Edwd TYDAY Mariner and Batch and Mary EDWARDS Spinr. Floyd

433.   7th. James PRESTWOOD of Wapping Mariner and Thomizen ELIOTT of Do. W; W

434.   7th. Wm. CUTHBERT of Wt Chapple Batchr and Sarah RIVET of Do. Spr Floyd

435.   8. Thomas CLARK of Stepney Weavr. and Elin. DURANT of Do. Spr

436.   11. Peter WOLFORD of Batersey Gardner
and Rose MANTHURST of Do. Batchr and Spinsr Floyd

437.   11th. James BOOCK of wt. fryers Waterman and Bat.
and Ann MARLOW of Do. Spinstr.

438.   11th. John COOK of St Giles in the field Cutler & Batr
& Ann THOMAS of St Andrews Holborn Spr. Floyd

Folio 23 verso

439.   August 11th 1728. Joseph ERICKE of St Sepulchers Br
and Dorothy ICE* of Do. Spr Floyd
*[*Possibly JEE]*

440.   12th. John BELL a Black Baptized p Floyd

441.   14th. John ELNER Batchr. & Elizth JEFFERIS Spr Floyd

442.   14. Edwd. SANDALL of St Savrs. Miller & B and Febe SLOUGHTON Do. wido Flod*
*[*Presumably Floyd]*

443.   14. John TREASURE of St Giles's Batch and Sallmash ENLY of Do. Spr Floyd

444.   14. Geo: FILLABROWN & Sarah PHILLIPS B S Floyd

445.   18. Francis BONNEY of St Giless Batch
and Elizth HOLINGSWORTH of do. S. Floyd

446.   18. Thomas HUMPHRY of Eaton Bridge*
and Mary WOOD of Crowhurst in Surry Spinsr Floyd
*[*Probably Edenbridge in Kent, which is very close to Crowhurst in Surrey]*

447.   19. Joseph WRIGHT of Hanover Sque. and Jane TOD of Do. B & Spr Floyd

448.   19. John FRENCH of St Anns Cook and Mary WALKER of St Ands* Floyd
*[*Probably St Andrews Holborn]*

449.   19. William SUGG & Mary BOYEN B & W

450.   19. Peter TEMPLET of Abbots Langley* Bat. and Joanah HUMBER of Do Spr Floyd
*[*In Hertfordshire]*

Folio 24 recto

451.   August 19th 1728. Charles GALLAGHAR of St Clements Dean
and Catherine GILL of Ditto B & S Floyd

452.   19. John TAYLOR of St Savrs. Batchr and Rachell OBRIAN of Do. Spr Floyd

453.   20. Robert LONDER of Stepney Mariner Br and Jane MURRY of Do wido Floyd

454.   20. Samuell HOVID of Stepney Weaver & Br.
and Sarah WELLS of Ditto Spinsr. Floyd

455.	20. Phillip CRONE of St Georges mariner & Br.
	and Dorothy SWALLOW of Do. Spinsr Floyd
456.	20. William BIGGS & Jane TANNER p Floyd
457.	23. Joseph MOST of New Castle under Line* Batand Mary TALBOT of Do. p Floyd
	*[*In Staffordshire]*
458.	24. Robert CAMBELL of St Jameses Westr Bat
	and Eliz MORGAN of do Spinster p Floyd
459.	25. William WALHEN* of Criplegate Clog Maker
	and Ann ILING** of Do spinster p Floyd
	*[*Possibly WALKEN. **Possibly KING]*
460.	25. Henry GILLE of Bishopgate wid
	and Elizth. WRIGHT of Shordit. Spinster p Floyd.

Folio 24 verso

461.	Agust. 25th 1728. Frances ATKINS of Uxbridge Mad*
	and Mary HARDWITCH of Do. Spinster p Floyd
	*[*An abbreviation for Middlesex]*
462.	25. Richard SHARP of Criplegate Bat. and Elizth. HALOWAY of Do. Sp. p Floyd
463.	25. John WILKS Rothors hill Joyner Bat and Mary BOWATOR of Do Widow p Floyd
464.	26. John EVANS of Clarkenwell Blacksmith
	and Margt MACKULLA of St Sepulkers wt out Widow p Floyd
465.	26. Pogsston STANDWICK of Covent Garden Bat and Gent
	and Mary MEARS Spinster p Floyd
466.	26. James CLAYTON of St Jameses Soldier Bat
	and Sarah JANFON* of Do. Spr p Floyd
	*[*Possibly JANSON]*
467.	28. Charls NEWBURY of St Catrins by Tower Batt
	and Sarah HALFHEAD of Do. Spinster p Floyd
468.	29. Thos. BARTLET of Wood Street Weaver Widr
	and Hanah COOK of Stephney Widow p Floyd
469.	30. Richd TORRINGTON of Cudhora Shew Maker and Bat
	and Mary RICHARDSON of Do. Spr. p Floyd
470.	Dennis MURPHU* Husbandman and Ann SYMS Spr p Floyd
	*[*Presumably a mistake for MURPHY. There is no specific date for this entry but the layout of the page suggests that the date is the same as the previous entry]*

Folio 25 recto

471.	September 2d 1728. John DAVIDSON and Ann FORD Bar. & Spr Floyd
472.	2. John MUGGLESTON of Stepney Mariner Ba
	[and] Elinor CIRBY of the same Spinster Floyd
473.	3. Richard BARTHOW* of St Martins in the Fields Engraver
	& Elinor SHAW of Do B & S Floyd
	*[*Possibly BARLHOW]*
474.	3. Thomas ANDERSON of St Cathrs. Mariner
	[and] Susanna FRITH of Do. Batch & Spinsr. Floyd
475.	4. Mathew WALKER of St Geos. Hanr. Square Batch
	[and] Mary TUDER of St Dunstins in ye East Spinsr. Floyd
476.	4. John COOKE of St Savrs Founder and Batch
	[and] Constant KILLING of the same Spinstr. Floyd
477.	5. Luke BASS of Bromley in Kent Batch & Elizth. MUNK of the same Spinster Floyd

478.   6. John ANSCOMB of Addington in Kent Batr
       [and] Alic WINTON of the same Spinstr Floyd
479.   7. Wiliam NEWMAN of West Grinsd in Sussx.
       [and] Bridget MACDANNAL of St Gile's B & Sp Floyd
480.   8. John EMERTON of Mortlake Waterman & Mary CIRWOOD of the same Wr & Wo.
481.   8. John LEWIN of St olives Surry Waterman
       [and] Grace WATSON of New Carstle under Line* Floyd
       [*In Staffordshire]

Folio 25 verso

482.   September 8th 1728. George LEWEAS* of Buckland Surry Bat
       [and] Sarah GODFREY of the same Spinstr Floyd
       [*The last letter is unclear]
483.   9. Thomas WILLSON of St Georges Martyr B
       [and] Alce BISBROWN of the same Spinsr Floyd
484.   10. Thomas ADGOE of St Geo: Waterman B
       [and] Mary STAPLES of St James's Spnr Floyd
485.   10. William ROWEL of St Giles's fields Bat
       [and] Mary MORGAN of the same Wido Floyd
486.   10. William GORMER of St Mary Newington
       [and] Francis BENFIELD of the same Spr Floyd
487.   10. Benja: WHITEMAN of Rygate* Batchr.
       [and] Sarah LINVEL of the same Spinster Floyd
       [*Probably Reigate in Surrey]
488.   10. Robert FORT of Rotherhith Mariner Br.
       [and] Mary FELOWS of St Georg. Spinstr. Floyd
489.   10. William BUCKINGHAM of Aynsom Oxen
       [and] Mary SWENLEMAN of Enfield Wr. & Wo. Floyd
490.   11. John BUCKMAN of St Mary's Newington
       [and] Margarett DUGLASS of Do. Br & Wo. Floyd
491.   11. James TIGAN* of Hartlepool Durham
       [and] Alce SMITH of the same Spinstr Floyd
       [*Possibly FIGAN]
492.   11. John BLONDAL of St Mary's Newin.
       [and] Elinor MORRIS of White Chapple B* Floyd
       [*The page has been damaged so that the record of the bride's condition has been lost]

Folio 26 recto

493.   September 12th 1728. John George JONES of St Savrs Southwk
       [and] Elizth. ALLINGTON of the same Spinstr Floyd
494.   12. Edward ROUND Waterman & widor [and] Elizth BARRETT Spinstr. Floyd
495.   12. George GRIFFIN of Ewell in Surry Widr
       [and] Ann NELE of Longditten Spinster Floyd
496.   12. Thomas CARVELL of Stepney Coachman
       [and] Mary GUILFORED of Do Bat & Wid Floyd
497.   12. William BUTSEL of Aldgate Batch and Sarah TATE of wt. Chapple Wido Floyd
498.   13. William COLLINGS of St James's Gent & B.
       [and] Mary HATTON of the same Spinster Floyd
499.   13. John EVERET of St Sepulchers Batchr
       [and] Alce SELLS of St Giles's Cripplegate Floyd

500. 13. Charles JACKSON of Stanwell Batch
[and] Elizth MACKBETH of St James's Westr Spr Floyd
501. 14. Samuel HAYWARD Mariner & Batch
[and] Elizth. DEACON of Wappin Spinsr. Floyd
502. 15. William KETHAM* of Cripplege. Batch & Elizth FULLER of Do widdow Floyd
[*Possibly KELHAM]

Folio 26 verso
503. September the 15 1728. William COOPER of St James's Gent B
[and] Jane MORGAN of the same Spinstr Floyd
504. 15. Peter GILES of St Giles's widr and Elizth BULLMORE of St Ann's Spr Floyd
505. 15. John DAY of Harrow Labr & Batr [and] Elizth GARDNER of Do wido Floyd
506. 15. Richard ARMSTEAD of wt Chap. wdr.
[and] Elinor DAWSON of Do. Spinster Floyd
507. 16. William BARTLETT of St Clemt Deans
[and] Margarett PITT of St James wdo Floyd
508. 16. Griffith GRIFFIS of Mongomery widr
[and] Mary JONES of Pembrook wido Floyd
509. 16. Joseph BAKER of Criplegate Batr & Elizth GOODACHER of Do. Spinsr. Floyd
510. 16. Cotton HOOD of St Geo: Southwo. Br
[and] Elizth KEWARDEN of Do wido Floyd
511. 16. James HANSCOMB of Tedington wr
[and] Francis ALLER of Apley do. wido. Floyd
512. 17. Thomas PALLET of Chese* Labr & B.
[and] Elizth POLLET of Do. Spinster Floyd
[*Probably Chelsea]

Folio 27 recto
513. September 17 1728. Henry SILKWOOD of Canterbury* widr
[and] Mary HINTON of White Chapple wido Floyd
[*In Kent]
514. 17. George and Francis Floyd
[This entry, with limited information, is part of entry 1 of the notebook in RG
7/563]
515. 17. Thomas SWEETING of Durham Batch
[and] Margarett HEND of Do. Spinster Floyd
[This entry is an abstract of entry 2 of the notebook in RG 7/563, but note that a
date and the spouses' conditions have been added, the bride's surname has been
incorrectly copied from HEAD, and their residence has been shortened from
Stockton (in Durham). A slightly different version of this entry also appears at
entry 628 below, dated 23 October 1728]
516. 17. William TANNER of St Savours South
[and] Jane BIGGS of the same Spinster Floyd
[This entry is an abstract of entry 3 of the notebook in RG 7/563, but note that
the groom's surname has been incorrectly copied from TURNER and that the date
and the bride's condition have been added. This entry also appears at entry 630
below, dated 23 October 1728]
517. 18. William ADDAMS of ye first Regmt. Gds.
[and] Mary CLIFFORD of St Giles's wido Floyd
[This entry does not originate from the notebook in RG 7/563]

518. 18. John BLACKBORN of St Caths. Mariner
[and] Ruth HUTTON of Do Spinster Floyd
[This entry is an abstract of entry 4 of the notebook in RG 7/563, but note the incorrect date]

519. 19. James KEY of Christ Church Batch [and] Bershiba SWEETMAN Spinster Floyd
[This entry is an abstract of entry 5 of the notebook in RG 7/563, but note the incorrect date and that the bride's name has been incorrectly copied from Bethia SWETMAN. This entry also appears at entry 706 below, dated August 1729]

520. 19. Samuel ALLINGHAM of Betswerth* B
[and] Eliner HUTCHINS of Godleyman Spinsr Floyd
[Probably Betchworth in Surrey. This entry is an abstract of entry 6 of the notebook in RG 7/563, but note the incorrect date and groom's condition]*

521. 19. John READEN of Beadworth Warwick
[and] Mary WHITEHEAD of Islington B & wdo Floyd
[This entry is an abstract of entry 7 of the notebook in RG 7/563, but note the incorrect date and groom's condition and that the groom's surname has been incorrectly copied from READER]

522. 20. John FLOOD Mariner of Wells* Batchr
[and] Mary HENFIELD of Do. Spinstr. Floyd
*[*In Somerset. This entry is an abstract of entry 8 of the notebook in RG 7/563, but note the incorrect date and that the groom's surname has been incorrectly copied from HOOD]*

523. 20. Frances PERKINS of Stoke in Buckinghshire. Batchlr
and Lydia RASH of Burnham in do. Spr. Floyd
[This entry is an abstract of entry 9 of the notebook in RG 7/563, but note the incorrect date and that the groom's surname has been incorrectly copied from PARKINS]

Folio 27 verso

524. September 20 1728. Joseph MARKS of Aldgate Batchr
[and] Jennet CAMPBELL of Do Spinstr R Row
[This entry is an abstract of entry 10 of the notebook in RG 7/563, but note the incorrect date and that 'R Row' has been incorrectly transcribed from 'R Bow', or the Rainbow]

525. 20. William MUNJON of Saba Mariner [and] Ann MORGAN of Do Spinstr. Floyd
[This entry is an abstract of entry 11 of the notebook in RG 7/563, but note that the groom's surname has been incorrectly copied from MUNYON and that his residence in the notebook, St Sa, or St Saviours, has been incorrectly copied as Saba in this entry]

526. 20. William WOOD of Godleyman Batr
[and] Ann PARRIS of Bamley near Gilfd*. Floyd
*[*Probably Guilford in Surrey. This entry is an abstract of entry 12 of the notebook in RG 7/563]*

527. 21. William STONE of Down in Kent [and] Ann BSCOTT* of Do. Spinstr
*[*A vowel seems to be missing from this name, but the entry is an abstract of entry 13 of the notebook in RG 7/563, in which the bride's surname is actually PESCOTT]*

528. 21. Robert WILLIAMS of Gravesend B
[and] Elizth CANTRILL of Perfleet Spinsr Floyd
[This entry is an abstract of entry 14 of the notebook in RG 7/563, but note that the spouses' conditions have been added]

529. 22. Richard STANLEY of St Botolphs [and] Jane JONES of Lambeth Spinster Floyd
      *[This entry is an abstract of entry 15 of the notebook in RG 7/563, but note that
      the bride's surname has been incorrectly copied from JAMES]*
530. 23. Charles RICHARDSON of Plishea Batr
      [and] Ann WITNEY of Do. Spinster Floyd
      *[This entry is an abstract of entry 16 of the notebook in RG 7/563, but note that
      the bride's Christian name has been incorrectly copied from Amy]*
531. 23. Michell SIMPSON of wt Chap Br [and] Jane DIXON of Do wido Floyd
      *[This entry is an abstract of entry 17 of the notebook in RG 7/563, but note that
      the groom's condition has been incorrectly copied]*
532. 23. Edward ADDINGTON of St James's Br
      [and] Jane BRADBURY of St Geo: HS Spr Floyd
      [This entry is an abstract of entry 18 of the notebook in RG 7/563]
533. 23. John ASHREMAN of Aldgate Batr [and] Jane DAVIS of St Johns wap Spr Floyd
      *[This entry is an abstract of entry 19 of the notebook in RG 7/563, but note that
      the groom's surname has been incorrectly copied from ACHREMAN]*

Folio 28 recto
534. September 23 1728. John HARPER of St Geo: Southwark
      [and] Mary CARREY of Stepney Spinstr Floyd
      *[This entry is an abstract of entry 20 of the notebook in RG 7/563, but note that
      the bride's surname has been incorrectly copied from CAREY]*
535. 23. Henry EMMERSON of Queenhith Br
      [and] Ann SIMMONS of Coleman S spinr Floyd
      *[This entry is an abstract of entry 21 of the notebook in RG 7/563, but note that
      the bride's condition has been added]*
536. 24. Edward THOMPSON of St Marys [and] Ann WALKER of Do. Spinster Floyd
      *[This entry is an abstract of entry 22 of the notebook in RG 7/563. St Marys was
      the parish church of Islington, which is noted as the spouses' residence in the
      notebook]*
537. 24. William HACLIN of Strutham in Surry
      [and] Mary SWENLAND of Croyden Spinsr
      *[This entry is an abstract of entry 23 of the notebook in RG 7/563, which is
      repeated at entry 62 of the notebook, and at entry 576 in this register. Note that
      the spouses' surnames have been incorrectly copied from HALLIN and
      SWEZLAND. A further version of this entry appears at entry 708 below, dated
      August 1729]*
538. 24. Humphry GOOPE of St Leo: Shoreditch [and] Elizth ORAM of Do. Spinstr
      *[This entry is an abstract of entry 24 of the notebook in RG 7/563, but note that
      the groom's surname has been incorrectly copied from GRAPE]*
539. 24. William SAWYER of Thorp Batchr [and] Jane WAKEFORD of Do Spinstr Floyd
      *[This entry is an abstract of entry 25 of the notebook in RG 7/563, but note that
      the groom's name has been incorrectly copied from William THOMARVER, a
      Sawyer, and the bride's residence has been changed from Woking to Thorp]*
540. 25. James WOOD of St Clements Deans [and] Ann WILLSON of Do. B & Spr Floyd
      [This entry is an abstract of entry 26 of the notebook in RG 7/563]
541. 27. George LANSDALE of Stanhope Bat [and] Margarett CURTIS of Do. wido Floyd
      [This entry is an abstract of entry 27 of the notebook in RG 7/563]
542. 28. John LEVERIDGE of St Bennets Ba [and] Febe BOZE of Do. spinster
      [This entry is an abstract of entry 28 of the notebook in RG 7/563]

543.   28. James WARD of Stepney Mariner
[and] Hannah UNDERWOOD of St James Clerkenwell & wido Floyd
[This entry is an abstract of entry 29 of the notebook in RG 7/563]

Folio 28 verso
544.   September 29th 1728. John ELLIS of St Leonards Sho. Dit*
[and] Ann RICH of Do. Batch & Spinsr Floyd
*[*This is short for Shoreditch. This entry is an abstract of entry 30 of the notebook in RG 7/563, but note that the spouses' conditions have been added and that the bride's surname has been incorrectly copied from REICH]*
545.   29. Rowland KING of Bexley in Kent [and] Mary WILLIAMS of do. Spinstr Floyd
[This entry is an abstract of entry 31 of the notebook in RG 7/563]
546.   29. Mathew LEE of St Mary wt. Chap. [and] Ann FRANKLIN of Do. Spinstr Floyd
[This entry is an abstract of entry 32 of the notebook in RG 7/563]
547.   29. John ROFEER of St Maryhill Batr
[and] Elizth. MURFIT of St olives Surr. wo. Floyd
[This entry is an abstract of entry 33 of the notebook in RG 7/563]
548.   29. Thomas LUCAS of St Marys wesn*
[and] Margarett STEPHENS of St Mary Lebon spinstr Floyd
*[*This is short for Westminster. This entry is an abstract of entry 34 of the notebook in RG 7/563, but note that the bride's condition has been added]*
549.   29. Miles CONNER of Enfield Batch [and] Hannah LAMBERT of St Martin Floyd
[This entry is an abstract of entry 35 of the notebook in RG 7/563]
550.   29. Thomas MATTOCKS of St Andr* B [and] Hannah DENT of Do. Spinsr Floyd
[St Andrews Holborn. This entry is an abstract of entry 36 of the notebook in RG 7/563]*
551.   30. Edward SAUNDERS of St Pauls Covt. Garden Batchlr and Vintner
and Mary HEALEY of St Andr* wido Floyd
*[*St Andrews Holborn. This entry is an abstract of entry 37 of the notebook in RG 7/563, but note that the bride's surname has been incorrectly copied from HEALE]*
552.   30. Henry HAYDON of east Tilbury Ex*. [and] Lydia BYFORD of Do. Spinstr Floyd
*[*This is short for Essex. This entry is an abstract of entry 38 of the notebook in RG 7/563]*
553.   30. Robt. GODDARD of St Savrs porter widr
[and] Barbary WHARTON of Do. Spinst. Floyd
[This entry is an abstract of entry 39 of the notebook in RG 7/563, but note that the groom's occupation of potter has been incorrectly copied as porter]

Folio 29 recto
554.   Septembr 30th 1728. Richard MARTIN of Darne in Kent
[and] Sarah WILLDAM of Willmington Spr Floyd
[This entry is an abstract of entry 40 of the notebook in RG 7/563]
555.   30. Richard JONES of Bosleham in Stafordshire Batchr
and Ann LEE of Haslemere in Surr* wdo Floyd
*[*This is short for Surrey. This entry is an abstract of entry 41 of the notebook in RG 7/563]*
556.   30. Andrew GOSHAM St Anne Batch [and] Mary JONES of folkston Kent spr Floyd
[This entry is an abstract of entry 42 of the notebook in RG 7/563]

557. October 1st 1728. John BROOKE of Brogsdon Batch
[and] Mary LYNSEY of Do. Spinstr. Floyd
[This entry is an abstract of entry 43 of the notebook in RG 7/563, but note that the groom's surname has been incorrectly copied from BROOKS. Brogsdon is in Hertfordshire, according to the notebook (it is probably an incorrect spelling of Broxbourne)]

558. 2. Thomas COLLIN of West Maldin Br [and] Mary SONG of Do. Spinstr Floyd
[This entry is an abstract of entry 44 of the notebook in RG 7/563, but note that the spouses' place of residence has been incorrectly copied from West Malling in Kent and that the bride's surname has been incorrectly copied from TONG]

559. 2. John JUDD of Yolding Kent Bat [and] Elizth BENNETT of Hanton Spinr Floyd
[This entry is an abstract of entry 45 of the notebook in RG 7/563, but note that the bride's place of residence has been incorrectly copied from Huntton]

560. 2. Thomas SAUNDERS by* Walton Batr
[and] Mary RICHARDSON of Do. Spinstr Floyd
[A mistake for 'of'. This entry is an abstract of entry 46 of the notebook in RG 7/563, but note that the groom's surname has been incorrectly copied from SANDERS]*

561. 2. William STILES of Rutham Batr [and] Mary FLOW of Do. spinstr. Floyd
[This entry is an abstract of entry 47 of the notebook in RG 7/563, but note that the bride's name has been incorrectly copied from Margaret HOW]

562. 3. William WALL of South frambridg* Bat [and] Mary SMITH of Do. Spinstr Floyd
*[This entry is an abstract of entry 48 of the notebook in RG 7/563, but note that the spouses' conditions have been added. *This is in Essex, according to the notebook]*

563. 3. Thomas PEWTRIS of Backin Batr
[and] Mary KELSHEW of Bromstead Spin. Floyd
[This entry is an abstract of entry 49 of the notebook in RG 7/563, but note that the spouses' places of residence have been incorrectly copied]

Folio 29 verso

564. October ye 3 1728. Francis HAYLOCK of Sisberry Ba
[and] Elizth HOOPER of Deptford Spinsr. Floyd
[This entry is an abstract of entry 50 of the notebook in RG 7/563, but note that the groom's place of residence has been incorrectly copied and that the bride's condition has been added]

565. 3. Thomas BURLIN of Stafford Bat [and] Mary STANER of Barkin Spr Floyd
[This entry is an abstract of entry 51 of the notebook in RG 7/563, but note that the bride's surname has been incorrectly copied from STANES]

566. 3. Jonathan LAUGHLIN of Lee Batr [and] Elizth FREEMAN of Do. Spinsr. Floyd
[This entry is an abstract of entry 52 of the notebook in RG 7/563]

567. 4. Ezekiah OGLE of Stepney Marinr [and] Mary GARDNER of Do. Batr & Wdo Floyd
[This entry is an abstract of entry 53 of the notebook in RG 7/563]

568. 4. John WALKIN of South fleet Batr [and] Mary BATES of Do Spinstr. Floyd
[This entry is an abstract of entry 54 of the notebook in RG 7/563, but note that the groom's surname has been incorrectly copied from WAKLIN]

569. 4. Thomas MILLS of Stepney Marrinr. [and] Elizth. BASFOOT of Do. Spinstr. Floyd
[This entry is an abstract of entry 55 of the notebook in RG 7/563, but note that the groom's surname has been incorrectly copied from MILES]

570. 5. John NUTS of St Giles's Batch [and] Jane DEAKERS of Do. Spinstr. Floyd
[This entry is an abstract of entry 56 of the notebook in RG 7/563, but note that the spouses' conditions have been added]

571. 6. Richard DUNMAN of Christ Church [and] Susanna SWERET of Do. W: W
[This entry is an abstract of entry 57 of the notebook in RG 7/563, but note that the groom's surname has been incorrectly copied from DUNMAR and that the bride's condition has been added]

572. 6. William GRAVET of Mitcham* widr [and] Margarett REED of Do wido Floyd
*[*In Surrey. This entry is an abstract of entry 58 of the notebook in RG 7/563, but note that the date has been incorrectly copied]*

573. 6. William GRAY of Stepney Marinr. [and] Isabela HARDOM of Do. Spinstr. Floyd
[This entry is an abstract of entry 59 of the notebook in RG 7/563, but note that the date has been incorrectly copied and that the groom's condition has been added]

574. 6. Edward HIVE of Shadwell Mar [and] Elizth ATKINS of Do. Bat & W
[This entry is an abstract of entry 60 of the notebook in RG 7/563, but note that the date has been incorrectly copied]

Folio 30 recto

575. October ye 6 1728. John HUTCHINS of the 1st Regt Gds
[and] Anna Maria HALL St Mart B: W
[This entry is an abstract of entry 61 of the notebook in RG 7/563, but note that the date has been incorrectly copied]

576. 6. William HALLIN Strutham* Br. [and] Mary SWENLAND of Do. Spinstr.
*[*Probably Streatham in Surrey. This entry is an abstract of entry 62 of the notebook in RG 7/563 (and repeats entry 537 above, and entry 23 in the notebook), but note that the date has been incorrectly copied. A further version of this entry appears at entry 708 below, dated August 1729]*

577. 6. Richard BARTON of St Andrews*
[and] Elinor MIARES of St Clemt Deans Sp Floyd
*[*St Andrews Holborn. This entry is an abstract of entry 63 of the notebook in RG 7/563, but note that the date has been incorrectly copied and that the bride's condition has been added]*

578. 6. William HINKLEY of Mitcham* Br [and] Mary FRANCIS of Do. Spinster
*[*In Surrey. This entry is an abstract of entry 65 of the notebook in RG 7/563]*

579. 7. William HAMMOND of Shoreham B.
[and] Jane LATTIC of Otford in Kent Spin Floyd
[This entry is an abstract of entry 66 of the notebook in RG 7/563, but note that the bride's surname has been incorrectly copied from LATTER]

580. 7. Samuel BENNETT of St Andrews* [and] Susanna DARBEY of St Giles's Sp Floyd
*[*St Andrews Holborn. This entry is an abstract of entry 68 of the notebook in RG 7/563]*

581. 7. Thomas BIRD of Ainsford Batr [and] Mary ALTRIP of Shorham Spinstr Floyd
[This entry is an abstract of entry 69 of the notebook in RG 7/563]

582. 7. Robt. SMALL of St Sepulchers Bat [and] Sarah MAYHEW Blackfryers Spr Floyd
[This entry is an abstract of entry 70 of the notebook in RG 7/563, but note that the groom's condition has been added]

583. 7. Geo: BRIGHTWELL Soler* & Batch
[and] Margarett BELL of St Martins Spr Floyd
*[*Soldier. This entry is an abstract of entry 71 of the notebook in RG 7/563, but note that the groom's surname is spelt differently]*

584.   8. Edward EDWARDS Wiltshire Ba.
        [and] Elizth. CANNING of St Gabriel Fan. Church Street Floyd
        [This entry is an abstract of entry 72 of the notebook in RG 7/563]

Folio 30 verso

585.   October 8 1728. Wm. SMITH son of John & Ann SMITH Baptized Octr Floyd
        *[This entry is an abstract of entry 199 of the notebook in RG 7/563, but note that
        the date and the name of the minister have been incorrectly copied]*
586.   8. Tobias GOBART of St Martins in ye fields Taylor and Batchlr
        and Mary CAWOOD of Do. Spinstr Floyd
        [This entry is an abstract of entry 73 of the notebook in RG 7/563]
587.   8. Henry RICHARDSON of St James's Clerkenwell Batch
        and Margt. WILLSON of the same Spinstr. Floyd
        [This entry is an abstract of entry 74 of the notebook in RG 7/563]
588.   8. Wm. HALBROW of St Anne Bt. [and] Elizabeth WHITECOAT of Do. Spr Floyd
        *[This entry is an abstract of entry 75 of the notebook in RG 7/563, but note that
        the spouses' place of residence has been incorrectly copied from 'St Sa', probably
        St Saviours]*
589.   8. George SPURHAM of St Sepul. Bt. [and] Elizth. CREED of St Giles's wido Floyd
        [This entry is an abstract of entry 76 of the notebook in RG 7/563]
590.   8. Wm. GIPSON of St Sepulchers Bat
        [and] Jane DORCAP of Clerkenwl. wido Floyd
        *[This entry is an abstract of entry 77 of the notebook in RG 7/563, but note that
        the bride's surname has been incorrectly copied from DORCASS]*
591.   10. James MARTIN of Longfield widr [and] Sarah BATH of Neastead Wido Floyd
        *[This entry is an abstract of entry 78 of the notebook in RG 7/563, but note that
        the bride's condition has been incorrectly copied]*
592.   11. John HOSGOOD of Craydon Batch [and] Ann SHAW of Alhollows Widow Floyd
        *[This entry is an abstract of entry 79 of the notebook in RG 7/563, but note that
        the groom's place of residence has been incorrectly copied from Crediton (in
        Devon)]*
593.   12. George WORRIL of Stepney Batr.
        [and] Elizth. STRAFORD of Newington Spr Floyd
        *[This entry is an abstract of entry 80 of the notebook in RG 7/563, but note that
        the bride's surname has been incorrectly copied from STRATFORD]*
594.   12. Arthur BULLMAN of St Lawr* [and] Mary EARLE of Do. Spinster Floyd
        *[*The rest of the name is obliterated by damage to the page. However, this entry
        is an abstract of entry 81 of the notebook in RG 7/563, which notes the parish as
        St Lawrence, Reading (in Berkshire), but as the parish of the bride only, not of the
        groom. The bride's condition has also been added in this entry]*

Folio 31 recto

595.   October ye 12 1728. Henry ICOMB of Stepney Batr
        [and] Ruth ASKLEY of Do. Spinster Floyd
        *[This entry is an abstract of entry 82 of the notebook in RG 7/563, but note that
        the groom's surname has been incorrectly copied from SCOMB, which was itself
        probably a mistake for SECOMB, and that the bride's surname has been
        incorrectly copied from ASHLEY]*
596.   12. George COX of Bishopsgt. Batr [and] Hester UFFORD of Shoreditch Spr Floyd
        [This entry is an abstract of entry 83 of the notebook in RG 7/563]

597. 13. Thomas WATERS of St Pauls widr. [and] Mary FOSTER St James's wido Floyd
[This entry is an abstract of entry 84 of the notebook in RG 7/563, but note that the bride's condition has been added]

598. 13. John BURNE of St Catr Batr [and] Mary HARDERWICK of Do. Spr Floyd
[This entry is an abstract of entry 85 of the notebook in RG 7/563, but note that the groom's condition has been added and that the bride's surname has been incorrectly copied from HADDERWICK]

599. 13. Thomas FIRTH of Shoreditch [and] Margt. ROBERTSON of Do. Spinr. Floyd
[This entry is an abstract of entry 86 of the notebook in RG 7/563]

600. 13. Robert CROWDIRS of Queenhith Br
[and] Hannah BENTLY of St Sepulr Spr Floyd
[This entry is an abstract of entry 87 of the notebook in RG 7/563]

601. 14. Daniel DAVIS of Lowlayton Batr [and] Elizth. PERRING of Do. Spinster Floyd
[This entry is an abstract of entry 88 of the notebook in RG 7/563]

602. 14. John ROUSE of Finchley Batchr [and] Mary SHAW of Deptford Spinstr. Floyd
[This entry is an abstract of entry 89 of the notebook in RG 7/563, but note that the groom's surname is spelt differently]

603. 14. John GROSS of Stepney Mariner wi
[and] Mary GILLAM of Limehouse wid Floyd
[This entry is an abstract of entry 90 of the notebook in RG 7/563, but note that the groom's condition has been added]

604. 14. John and Martha Floyd
[No further information is provided about this couple. This entry is an abstract of entry 91 of the notebook in RG 7/563, which also omits the spouses' surnames (for the reason stated there)]

Folio 31 verso

605. October ye 14 1728. Mathew WALKER of St Georges Batr
[and] Sarah SAVAGE St Savrs. Spinstr. Floyd
[This entry is an abstract of entry 92 of the notebook in RG 7/563]

606. 14. Richard GARDNER and Elizabeth SEDWICK Floyd
[This entry does not originate from the notebook in RG 7/563]

607. 15. Thomas LARK wt. Chappl. Batr [and] Elinor GARDNER of Do. Wido Floyd
[This entry is an abstract of entry 93 of the notebook in RG 7/563]

608. 15. John LAWALLEY of Covt. Gard Br.
[and] Elinor WENTWORTH of Do. Spinr Floyd
[This entry is an abstract of entry 94 of the notebook in RG 7/563, but note that the groom's Christian name has been incorrectly copied from James]

609. 15. John JOHNSON of ye 2d Regt Foot B
[and] Mary SMITH of Aldgate Spinsr Floyd
[This entry is an abstract of entry 95 of the notebook in RG 7/563]

610. 15. Samul. BECH of St Giles's Batch [and] Mary DEMAN of Do. Spinster Floyd
[This entry is an abstract of entry 96 of the notebook in RG 7/563]

611. 17. Henry FLOUDGATE of St Geo: widr
[and] Mary BARNS of wt. Chapl. wido Floyd
[This entry is an abstract of entry 97 of the notebook in RG 7/563]

612. 17. William TAYLER of St Andrew* Br
[and] Sarah REDHEAD of Stepney Spinr Floyd
*[*St Andrews Holborn. This entry is an abstract of entry 98 of the notebook in RG 7/563, but note that the groom's surname is spelt differently]*

613.   17. Edward HOLMES of Darby Bat [and] Elizth WHITE of St Giles's Spinr Floyd
       *[This entry is an abstract of entry 99 of the notebook in RG 7/563. See the note to
       that entry as to the date of this marriage]*
614.   17. William COLEY of Cripl. Gate Bat. [and] Hannah BAGLEY of Aldersg. Sp. Floyd
       *[This entry is an abstract of entry 100 of the notebook in RG 7/563. See the note
       to that entry as to the date of this marriage]*

Folio 32 recto October ye 20th 1728.
615.   John DAVIS of Stepney Mar & B [and] Elizth. MASON of Do. Spinster Floyd
       [This entry is an abstract of entry 102 of the notebook in RG 7/563]
616.   20. Thomas CRISWELL of St Maudlins B [and] Ann BULY of Do. Spinstr Floyd
       *[This entry is an abstract of entry 104 of the notebook in RG 7/563, but note that
       the groom's surname is spelt differently and that the groom's condition has been
       added. A slightly different version appears at entry 717 below, dated 20 October
       1729]*
617.   20. Thomas WILLIAMS of Clerkw. Wdr. [and] Jane SMITH of Do widow Floyd
       [This entry is an abstract of entry 105 of the notebook in RG 7/563]
618.   21. James REVE of Pitsey widr [and] Martha WARNER of Bently wido. Floyd
       *[This entry is an abstract of entry 106 of the notebook in RG 7/563. See the note
       to that entry as to the date of this marriage]*

Folio 32 verso October 22 1728
619.   Samuel ELWOOD of ye 1 Regmt of Guards Bat
       and Eliz WILLMOTH of the parish of St Olives Sp married in ye Mint*
       *[*The Mint was not in the Fleet, but in Southwark (see the introduction to this
       volume). This entry is an abstract of entry 204 in the notebook in RG 7/563,
       which appears to be dated 18 December 1728]*
620.   Nicholas BARBER staymaker of Pipe River
       & Mary RUSLON of Kings Bromley Br. Spr.
621.   Thomas HALL of shadwell mariner & Jane TURNER St Olives w w
       [This entry is repeated at entry 658 below, dated December 1728]
622.   John HOPKINS of St Mary white Chapel Butcher
       & Ann WOODHEAD of Stepney Br Spr

Folio 33 recto October 23 1728
623.   Will FHREEVES of St Botolphs algate Bat
       and Martha MUNDAY Spinster Ditto Wagstaff mineter*
       *[*Minister]*
624.   Thomas LANE of Swan Alley Clarkenwell par. Carman
       & Elizth CLARK of St Andrews Holbourn Wr. W
625.   Richard EATON Gent Sarvt & Bat of St Marys Lebo & Mary PIRONIE* Sp
       *[*This name is written in very small handwriting and is almost illegible]*
626.   Robert DUNBARR of St Mary Rotherhith Marr. & Elizth. HAMELL Do Br. Spr.
627.   Erasmus NORWICH of Cripelgate Gent
       & Mary OLLERHEAD of St Stephen Coleman street Br. Spr.

Folio 33 verso. October 23 1728
628.   Thomas SWEETING and Margaret HEAD Stockton in Barck Shire B: S
       *[This entry is a slightly different version of entry 515 above. The reference to
       Berkshire appears to be an error]*

629.   Henry BAILEY of St Botolphs Bishops gate weaver & Ester LOTON Do Br Spr
630.   William TANNER
       and Jane BIGS of St Saviours Southwark in Bird Age walk*
       at Carbets
       *[*Presumably a mistake for Bird Cage Walk. This entry is a slightly different
       version of entry 516 above]*
631.   Joseph JERVIS of Aldgate High street marr. & Mary GILLETT Do Br Spr

Folio 34 recto. October 24 1728

632.   John HOUGDH* Gent of St martins in ye fields
       and Jennet GOSLIN of St Margret west B: S
       *[*Probably a mistake for HOUGH]*
633.   Richd. VAUGHAN of Covent Garding Barber Surgeon
       & Ann SMITH of St Brides Br Spr
634.   Gilbert BURTON Bat & Alice FLEMING or BRUCE*
       *[*The bride may have been a widow, so these surnames may be both her maiden
       and married names]*
635.   Willm. THOMPSON of Stepney Butcher
       & Frances SIMPSON of St Margrets westminster Br W

Folio 34 verso. October 1728

636.   George EDMONDS of X Chr Spittle fields Pumpmaker & Elizth BOURN Do Br. Spr.
637.   John LINTON of St Giles Cripelgate Ostler & Mary STEVENS Do Br. Spr.
638.   Edwd HOLMES of St Giles ye fields Gent Servt & Ann JERVIS Br. Spr.
639.   Willm. REYNOLDS of Coleman street Painter & Martha BECK Br. Spr

Folio 35 recto. November 1 1728

640.   Thos MOUNTAIN of X Chr. Newgate Street Cordwr
       [and] Susanah INWOOD of St Botolphs Aldersgate Br. Spr
641.   William BRADFIELD of St Georges Queen Square Gent and Bat & Eliz KINDELL Sp
642.   Peter NICHOLS of Newington Kent Flax Dresser & Mary GOODING Do Wr. W
643.   Thos. HUDSON of St Margts westmr House Carpenter
       & Sarah PARSONS Do Br Spr
644.   John EVERTON St George Southwk Baker & Susanah COLLINGS Br. W

Folio 35 verso. November 1728

645.   Goat*. Charls SPEED of Horsly down marriner & Batt and Jane WEST Sp Floyd
       *[*From this point in the register, many of the entries commence with the name of
       the tavern or marriage house in which the ceremony took place]*
646.   Goat. James WATMAN Butcher of St Ann Soho and Mary GREEN B S
647.   2. at Goat. Stephen MUCKELROY of St James westminst Bat & Saddler
       & Marrgret*
       *[*No further details of the bride are noted]*

Folio 36 recto November 1728

648.   Goat: Robert DOWNS of new Brandford Brickmaker and Ann MATHEWS Do B W
649.   at Shaw. Samuell HILL* of Stepney marriner & Sarah ALLEN Do B. W
       *[*Possibly BILL]*
650.   at Whit: John STEWDLY of Leatherhead* Hub man and Jane MARLEY Ditto B Sp
       *[*In Surrey]*

Folio 36 verso November 1728

651.   11. Henry BATTEN of Stepney mariner & Bat
       & Mary WOODHAM Spinster at mrs. Wilsons J F min
       [This entry is an abstract of entry 156 in the notebook in RG 7/563]

652.   11. Richard STENNETT of Wotton neare Darkin* wido & Husb
       & Eliz LIPSCOMBE Do Wilsons J F
       *[*Dorking in Surrey. This entry is an abstract of entry 157 in the notebook in RG
       7/563]*

653.   11. Joseph LEAK of St Marys white Chappel Clockmaker & Wido
       & Joanna HOWIT Do widow at mrs wilsons Floyd
       [This entry is an abstract of entry 158 in the notebook in RG 7/563]

Folio 37 recto December 1728

654.   at Bennetts'. John JENKINSON of Xth. Church London
       and Eliz ORTON of St Mathews Fryday Street B Sp
       [This entry does not specify the exact date]

655.   Steend* Will HENLEY of Stepney marrier & Jane OXLAD of Alesford B W
       [*The name is unclear. This entry does not specify the exact date]

Folio 37 verso December 1728

656.   Benjamin MORGEN of St Botolph Aldgate Bat & mariner
       & Jane GREEN Ditto at Clifton Floyd
       [This entry does not specify the exact date]

657.   John MARTIN of St Leonords Shore Ditch
       and Eliz GODDARD Ditto Sp at the Barly mowe Floyd
       *[This entry does not specify the exact date. It is an abstract of entry 186 in the
       notebook in RG 7/563, dated 21 November 1728]*

Folio 38 recto December 1728

658.   Whit. Thomas HALL of Shadwell marrier & Jane TURNER of St Olaves W: W
       *[This entry does not specify the exact date. It repeats entry 621 above, dated 22
       October 1728]*

659.   Shaw. Thomas HOLDEN and Eliz BLEWITT 17 Nov last not to be destored*
       *[*I cannot say what this means, but it is possibly a note that the entry should not
       be disclosed to others. This entry specifies the date of 17 November 'last', but
       appears in a section for marriages of December. This suggests that the ceremony
       had taken place a month earlier and the minister only remembered to record it in
       December 1728]*

Folio 38 verso December 1728

660.   Coffee house. Will WARRIN of St Giles in the fields Bat & Ann MAY Sp
       [This entry does not specify the exact date]

661.   Motts. William PATRICK of St Andrews Holborn Bat & Taylor
       and Eliz FARRMER Sp Thos Ryder
       [This entry does not specify the exact date]

662.   John LARK of St Martins in ye fields Cord Bat and Mary TRUEMAN widow T Ryder
       [This entry does not specify the exact date]

Folio 39 recto January 1 1729

663. Coffee house. Dominiro WITALL of St Johns Wapping mariner
and Sarah PARIS Ditto B Sp

664. Mott. Thomas POTTER St Martins in ye fields Gent
and Mary BOMAN of the same B Sp

Folio 39 verso. January 1729

665. Whit. Richard MOUTH of St Martins in the fields and Mary MARTIN Sp Thos Ryder
[This entry does not specify the exact date]

666. Stacy. William WEST of St Martin in the fields Bat & Taylor and Mary PICTMAN* Sp
[*Possibly PICKMAN. This entry does not specify the exact date]

Folio 40 recto. January 1729

667. Whit. Richard PAINE of St Pauls Shadwell
& Mary THROSLEY of St Saviours Southwark W W
[This entry does not specify the exact date]

668. Stacy. Will WARWICK of Stratford in Essex Gent Sarvt
& Rachel CORNER of St Anns Soho B Sp
[This entry does not specify the exact date]

Folio 40 verso. January 1729

669. Henry MORRIS solier* and Eliz JONES Sp at mr. Cliftons Floyd
[*Probably a soldier. This entry does not specify the exact date]

670. Jonthan HOPWOOD of Luisham* and Mary SPENCER wido & widow Floyd
*[*Lewisham in Kent. This entry does not specify the exact date. It is an abstract of
entry 198 in the notebook in RG 7/563, dated 8 December 1728]*

Folio 41 recto. Febary 1729

671. Whit. Robert HOLLAND Barnett Baker & Ann GARY Do B Sp
[This entry does not specify the exact date]

672. Goat. Will ENGLAND of Batersea Gardner & Eliz TAYLER w. sp
[This entry does not specify the exact date]

Folio 41 verso. Feb 1729

673. 5. John HOWARD of Harrow on ye Hill Husb
and Sarah WOOD Br. Sp James Wagst.

Folio 42 recto. Februry 1729

674. Queens Head Stacy*. Thomas GREEM** of Teddington Husb
& Mary OSBAND of hampton
*[*Stacy is the name of the minister. **This may be a mistake for GREEN. The
entry does not specify the exact date]*

675. Whit. Joseph GOODMAN of St Mary le Bowe vitualer and Mary YONGE Ditto B Sp
[This entry does not specify the exact date]

Folio 42 verso Febr 1729.

676. Davy BEDFORD Bat of Graseing in Kent [and] Mary GERINOTT Clwalker*
[*This word is unclear. The entry does not specify the exact date]

677.   Richard ROWE of St James Westm Labr and Bat [and] Hannah WEAVER Sp Floyd
        [This entry does not specify the exact date]

Folio 43 recto March 1729
678.   Whit. Stacy. Robert BRUDENELL of St Clements Danes Prushmaker*
        and Alice ELLIS of St Giles W W
        *[*Probably a mistake for brushmaker. The entry does not specify the exact date. A
        further version of this entry appears at entry 720 below, dated November 1729]*
679.   Whit. Henry LAWRENCE of Clarkenwell Labr & Eliz BARBER of St Martins B Sp
        [This entry does not specify the exact date]

Folio 44 recto March 1729
680.   Wills. George IRELAND of Covent Garden Cook
        & Mary SIMPSON of St Georges in fields W Sp Stacy
        [This entry does not specify the exact date]
681.   Barbers. Will STREET of fullham Brickmaker & Eliz JORDEN Do B sp
        [This entry does not specify the exact date]

Folio 45 recto April 1729
682.   Whits. George MARRIOTT of Criplegate Hartshorn Rasper
        and Esther WAYLAND Ditto B Sp Stacey
        [This entry does not specify the exact date]
683.   Kings armes. Thomas CHAPPELL of Criplegate Gent
        & Martha WHYVELL of White Chappell Stacy
        [This entry does not specify the exact date]

Folio 45 verso April 1729
684.   Edward SANDERS of St James Clarkenwell Bat and Mary MORRIS Sp
        [This entry does not specify the exact date]

Folio 46 recto May 1729
685.   Queens head. Henry GARDINER of St andrews* Cane Chairmaker
        [and] Ann TAYLER of St Giles W: W Mr Mottram
        [*Probably St Andrews Holborn. This entry does not specify the exact date]
686.   Whits. Richard CLIVE of Stick in ye County of Salop Gent
        and Rebettah GASKILL of St Austins B Spinster Stacy
        [This entry does not specify the exact date]

Folio 46 verso May 1729
687.   John WHILER of St Pauls Shadwell marr Bat and Elizabeth PUMER Sp
        [This entry does not specify the exact date]
688.   William COVENTERY of St Martins in ye fields Bat and Mary SANDERS Sp
        [This entry does not specify the exact date]
689.   Tho. PARSON of St James Clarkenwell Cord B & Ann PUE
        [This entry does not specify the exact date]

Folio 47 recto June 1729
690.   Whits. John LATHUM of Aldgate Dyer & Ann HALL Do B Sp
        [This entry does not specify the exact date]

691.   Whits. Will RIVERES of Frimley in Surry Gardner & Eliz BETTS Do
        [This entry does not specify the exact date]

Folio 47 verso June 7 1729
692.   7. WESTID John* of St Marys overs Taylor & Bat and Ann SPARKES Spinster
        [*This entry (and the following two entries) include the groom's surname before his Christian name]
693.   8. WOOTEN John of St Martins in the fields Cord Bat & Mary FARMER Spinster
694.   12. MURPHY Tho of St Martins in ye fields Taylor Bat and Eliz WARSAR Spinster

Folio 48 recto June 1729
695.   Goat. Will HUMPHREY of Hamstead miller
        and Martha WEIDEN of Edgeborough in Bucks B Sp Stacy
        [This entry does not specify the exact date]
696.   Goat. John ENGLAND of Wakefielde in Yorkshire Clothworker
        and Eliz BEDDALL of St Brides B W
        [This entry does not specify the exact date]

Folio 48 verso July 1729
697.   Thomas WARD of St Martin in the fields Cord Bat and Eliz FURTICUE Spinster
        [This entry does not specify the exact date]
698.   Edward PALMER of St Climon Deans Taylor & Bat & Mary FOX Sp
        [This entry does not specify the exact date]

Folio 49 recto. July 1729
699.   Goat. Thomas WOODIN Eltham* Husbman & Eliz PLAN ditto B Sp
        [*In Kent. This entry does not specify the exact date]
700.   Whit. Will ADAMS of Aldgate Stocking Weaver & Sarah WOODLAND Ditto B Sp
        [This entry does not specify the exact date]
701.   Whit. Abraham ROLLES of St Giles Carver & Judeth CONNYER ditto Bat Sp
        [This entry does not specify the exact date]

Folio 49 verso July 1729
702.   Thomas THOMPSON Bat and Martha BREWER
        [This entry does not specify the exact date]
703.   James WOOD of St Clement Bat Frutir & Ann WILLSON Sp
        [This entry does not specify the exact date]

Folio 50 recto August 1729
704.   Whit. Thomas DAVIS of St James Westm Gent Sarvt
        and Eliz CAMPBELL W W Stacy
        [This entry does not specify the exact date]
705.   Coffee house. Daniel PEARRE St Margt Westm Plaeter
        and Rebette WILIAMS Ditto B W p Mottram
        [This entry does not specify the exact date]

Folio 50 verso August 1729

706.   James KEY of Crist Church Surry Bat & Turner
and Bethia SWETMAN of St Clement Deans Sp Floyd
[This entry does not specify the exact date. It is a slightly different version of entry 519 above]

707.   John HOOD of the Citty of Wells* mariner & Bat
and Mary HINFIELD Sp at Mr Wittons Whetshaef Floyd
[*In Somerset. This entry does not specify the exact date]

708.   William HALLIN of the Par of Strutham in Surry Bat
and Mary SWERCAND of the Parish of Croyden mariner Spinster
[This entry does not specify the exact date, but it is a slightly different version of entries 537 and 576 above]

Folio 51 recto August 1729

709.   Whit. Edward BUTLER of Richmond* Gardner and Mary LOYD B Sp
[*In Surrey. This entry does not specify the exact date]

710.   Wills. Samuel CROWDER of Stanwell moor Papermaker
and Eliz LINTELL Ditto B Sp Evans
[This entry does not specify the exact date]

Folio 51 verso Sep 1729

711.   Arther COMBRIDG of St Andrews Holborn Bat
and Hannah WALKER widow D Wigmore
[This entry does not specify the exact date]

Folio 52 recto Sept 1729

712.   Whit. John COWDWELL of St Anns Soho Chireman*
and Ann SMITH St James Westm B Sp Stacy
[*Presumably a chairman. This entry does not specify the exact date]

713.   Whit. Robart TURLINGTON of Stepney Weaver
& Temporance SMITH of St Giles Cripplegate B: W
[This entry does not specify the exact date]

Folio 52 verso September 1729

714.   Joseph WATER Bat and of St Dunstans in ye West
& Mary PRICHARD Sp D Wigmore
[This entry does not specify the exact date]

Folio 53 recto Octr 1729

715.   Whit. Thomes WYMENT of St Anns Soho Tayler & Eliz SHARWOOD Do B Sp
[This entry does not specify the exact date]

716.   Goat. Edward WAINE of Kentsford in GlosterShire Lab
& Margarett CROWSER of Harksum in Northumberland W: Sp
[This entry does not specify the exact date]

Folio 53 verso October 20 1729

717.   20. Thomas CRISWELL of St martin Bat & Ann BULY Spinster Floyd
[This entry is a slightly different version of entry 616 above]

Folio 54 recto November 1729

718.   Whit. Ralph ROTHERHAM of Coleman Street Tayler
and Catherine CHARRETON Do Br Sp
[This entry does not specify the exact date]

719.   Wills. Charles FISHER of Woodford* Joyner and Margt RICHARDS St Oloves B Sp
*[*In Essex. This entry does not specify the exact date]*

Folio 54 verso Novb. 1729

720.   Whit. Robert BRUDENELL of St Clements Danes pruck* maker
& Alice ELLES St Giles W: W
*[*Probably a mistake for peruke or brush. This entry does not specify the exact
date. It is a slightly different version of entry 678 above]*

721.   Whit. Anthony HENKES* of St Giles Camp Distiler and Eliz YEOMANS Ditto W Sp
*[*This name is unclear. The entry does not specify the exact date]*

Folio 55 verso December 21: 1729

722.   Peter WILLIAMS Esq of Place Jenkin in the County of Denbigh
and Jane DAVIS of Ditto Sp Floyd

723.   John EDWARDS of St Giles Crp Gate mariner & Joyner Bat
& Sarah RENNOLDS Do Sp at mrs. Willsons Floyd
*[This entry is an abstract of entry 180 in the notebook in RG 7/563, dated 18
November 1728]*

Folio 56 recto December 1729

724.   James JOHNSTONE of the Precinct of Bridwell Bat and Peruckmaker
and Mary CAWARD Ditto Sp at the White Hares neare Holb Bridge Floyd
[This entry does not specify the exact date]

725.   Timothy NEWBERRY of St olives in Surry marchant Bat
and Lydia BAGLY Ditto Sp at mr Carbetts Floyd
*[This entry does not specify the exact date. It is an abstact of entry 178 in the
notebook in RG 7/563, dated 17 November 1728]*

End of register in RG 7/3

Register of Marriages in piece RG 7/163

From January 1736/37 to June 1740

This register is described in the PRO class list as consisting of only nine folios, but containing 'private' marriages of January 1737 to June 1740 conducted by the minister Wyatt.

The register has a PRO binding about 11 inches by 7 inches. This contains a paper booklet of 10 folios (the front cover of the booklet being folio 1). A sheet of paper (stamped as folio 11) has been added with the binding, but is blank. Folios 1 verso, 2 verso, 3 recto, 4 verso and 8 verso are also blank. On the front cover of the original register (folio 1 recto) is a label with '226' in typescript and another label with 'Fleet Marriages 146' in manuscript. The following manuscript also appears on the front cover:

> *Marriages by W.W containing ye Month of January, February 1736–7, Feb. 37–8 and April, May, June, July, August, September, October, November, December 1738, January, February, March 1738, April, May, June, July, October, November, December 1739, January, February, March 1739–40, April, June 1740 done at sundry places all untranscrib'd.*

An abstract of the entries in this register is set out below. The register does not include an index and the entries are not numbered. I have therefore given numbers to each entry in the abstract for ease of reference. The register contains 119 marriages and is particularly interesting because so many of the grooms are described as 'Gent', that is gentleman, and because a number of entries note that a backdated certificate of the marriage was issued to the couple.

The manuscript title on the cover notes that the marriages were performed by 'W.W' and many of the pages in the register are headed 'Out of W.W' or 'Out of W.Wy' (see for example illustration 5 on page 66). These are references to one of the most notorious of the Fleet parsons; Walter Wyatt. He conducted marriages in the Fleet, according to Burn, from 1713 to 1749 or 1750. He received very substantial fees from the many ceremonies that he performed and was perhaps only overtaken in his income from marriage fees by Dr Gaynam. Wyatt's notebooks of October 1748 record that the fees that he received, in that month alone, amounted to more than £57. Wyatt described himself as 'Mr Wyatt, Minister of the Fleet' and conducted many marriages at the Two Sawyers, on the corner of Fleet Lane and at the Hand and Pen, near Holborn Bridge. Others attempted to trade on Wyatt's reputation and sign; Joshua Lilley kept a marriage house named the Hand and Pen near Fleet Bridge and Matthias Wilson kept a house with the same sign on the bank of Fleet Ditch.

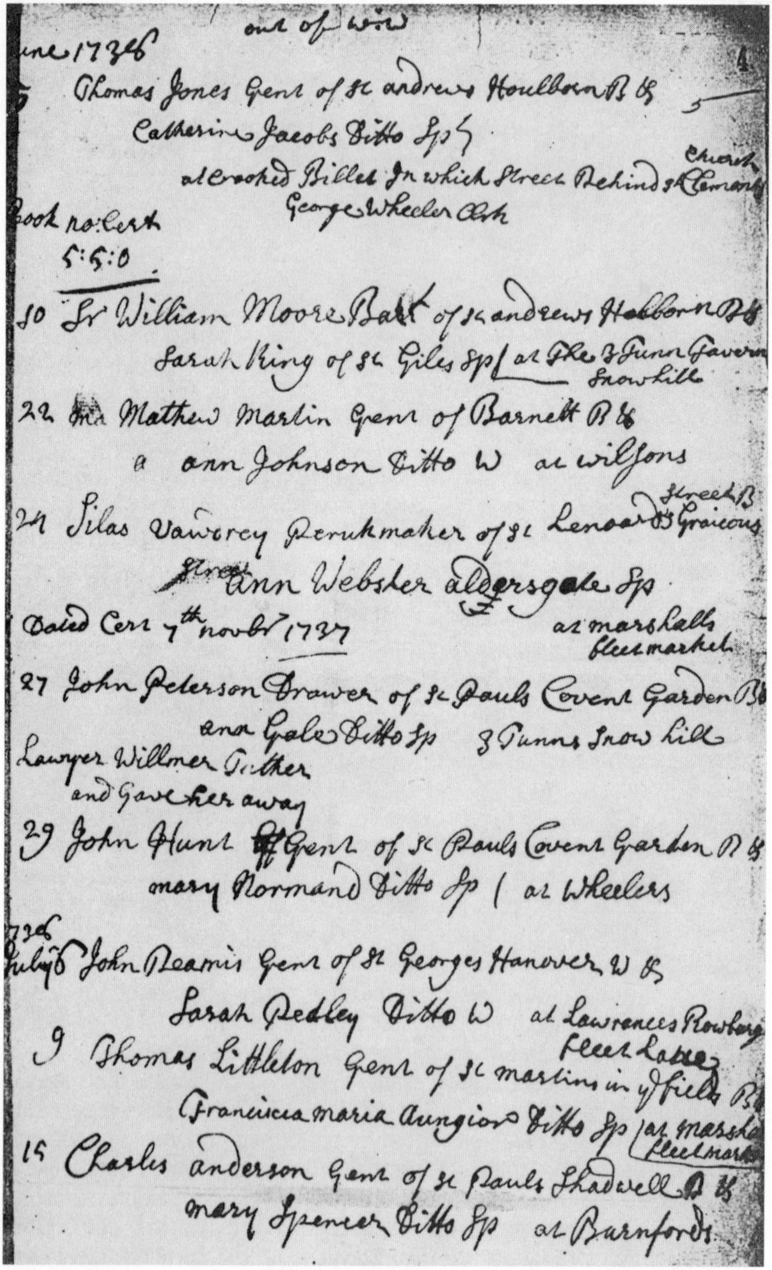

Illustration 5. A page (folio 4 recto) from the register in piece RG 7/163; marriages of 5 June 1738 –15 July 1738

Ashton (whose work is noted in the introduction to this volume) notes that Wyatt recorded various moral reflections in his notebooks. In one, he wrote:

The fear of the Lord is the beginning of wisdom,
The marrying in the Fleet is the beginning of eternal woe

In another notebook, Wyatt recorded the following words:

Give to every man his due and learn ye way of truth.
This advice cannot be taken by those that are concerned in ye Fleet marriages;
Not so much as ye Priest can do ye thing that is just and right there,
Unless he designs to starve.
For by lying, bullying and swearing,
To extort money from the silly and unwary people,
You advance your business

Wyatt died in 1750. His will, proved in the Prerogative Court of Canterbury, notes that he had an estate at Oxford, presumably purchased from the fees of his lucrative trade.

The entries in this register are, in my opinion, all in the same hand. This handwriting can be seen in illustration 5, which is a copy of folio 4 recto from the register, with entries (that I have numbered 15–23 in the following abstract) of June and July 1738. All the entries in RG 7/163 therefore appear to have been made by the same person. They were probably made within a short period of time, even though the entries cover a period of over three years.

The references to 'Out of W.W' may simply mean 'by W.W' (and that the register was compiled by Wyatt himself) or they may mean that the entries for the marriages were extracted from Wyatt's notebooks (of marriages at various places) by another person. The statement in the title on the front cover that these marriages were 'done at sundry places [and] all untranscrib'd' supports the latter suggestion (and is the reason that the PRO class list states that this register contains 'private' marriages). Entries 86 and 87 in the following abstract also suggest that someone other than Wyatt prepared this register. If Wyatt had been writing those entries into this register, he is unlikely to have written 'don't say where' in the space that was used for the marriage house at which the ceremony took place. He would have written 'I do not remember where' or something similar. Since the register is all in the same hand, it is therefore likely that all the entries were copied by someone else (probably from Wyatt's notebooks). It may be that someone discovered that these entries had been omitted when Wyatt's notebooks were copied into registers.

It is uncertain why many (perhaps all) of these entries were not transcribed into the larger registers. Many of the grooms appear to have been wealthy and so they may have requested confidentiality (and perhaps paid an extra fee for this service). Indeed, Wyatt noted specifically that nobody was 'to see the book' for the entry of the marriage of Thomas Clark and Mary Young on 2 March 1739/40 (entry 71).

The PRO class list states that this register covers marriages of January 1737 to June 1740. This is correct, except for one entry of July 1727 (entry 90). However, there are gaps in the period covered and the entries are not all in chronological order. The first page of the register (entries 1–7) features entries of January and February 1736/7 (that is 1736 in the Old Style of dating but 1737 in the New Style). There is then a jump to February 1737/8 (entry 8) and a further gap until April 1738 (entries 9–11). The entries then run chronologically to December 1738 (entry 51), except for entry 34 (December 1739). Entries 52–79 are a chronological sequence for December 1739 to June 1740. Finally, entries 80–119 are in chronological order, for January 1738/9 to November 1739, except for the rogue entry 90 (of July 1727).

Most of the entries in this register record the name of the tavern or marriage house at which the ceremony was performed. For example, there are references to the Three Tuns Tavern on Snow Hill (entries 3, 16, 19), the Hoop Tavern in Fleet Market (entries 12, 13), the interestingly named Whors Inn (entry 108) and Wheeler's, Boyce's, Lilly's and Wilson's marriage houses. Some marriages took place outside of the Rules of the Fleet, for example at the Temple (entry 36), at an apothecary's premises behind the Royal Exchange (entry 116) and at Tarrell's Bagnio in Long Acre (entry 33). A bagnio was a bath house (and often a brothel).

Wyatt was clearly happy to issue marriage certificates with false dates (or note a false date in the register of a marriage house). He also noted when he did so, although it is impossible to say whether he noted all the instances of this deception. This register notes that he provided backdated certificates on nine occasions (entries 18, 32, 38, 58, 70, 73, 84, 103 and 107).

Spouses came from all over Britain or even further afield to be married in the Fleet. The vast majority of spouses came from London or those counties, such as Essex and Surrey, which were close to London. However, many spouses (or couples) came from other English counties, or from other parts of the British Isles. This register records the marriage of William Thornboroughs, a gentleman from Northington in Southampton marrying Ann Duglas (or Douglas) of Mitcham in Surrey, probably on 1 May 1738 (entry 14). On 8 October 1738, James Clayton, a gentleman from Chichester in Sussex married Ann Parker of the same city at the Fountain, near St Sepulchres Church (entry 40). On 17 October 1739, John Collison, a gentleman from Sunderland, married Susanna Hicks at Boyce's marriage house (entry 112).

Many classes of people married in the Fleet. However, in contrast to most other registers, this register contains a higher proportion of professional men and gentlemen, but very few artisans or labourers. Gentlemen are the grooms in 78 of the 119 entries (for example entries 1, 2, 4, 9, 14, 15, 17 and 20). Entry 16 records the marriage of a baronet, or at least someone purporting to be a baronet (since I cannot find him in the standard reference works). Many professional men feature in this register; attorneys (entries 3 and 83), surgeons (entries 7, 98 and 115), an apothecary (entry 51) and goldsmiths (entries 43 and 84).

There are only two farmers (entries 42 and 50) and one sailor (entry 90). The only soldier is also noted as a gentleman (entry 77) and was undoubtedly an officer. Four of the grooms were gentlemens' servants or cooks (entries 11, 12, 67 and 92).

Some entries note the presence of witnesses, clerks or others. Ann Gale is noted as having been given away by a lawyer when she married John Peterson on 27 June 1738 (entry 19). Captain Mackphedre is recorded as having been present at the marriage of Edward Gilbec and Ann Knight on 24 July 1738 (entry 24). Edward Umfrevill was present at the marriage of William Umfrevill and Mary Weld in the Temple on 21 September 1738 (entry 36). The clerks George Wheeler, Jon. Crosier and Matt Wilson were recorded as present at marriages on 5 June 1738, 10 February 1738/9 and 30 June 1739 (entries 15, 88 and 101).

I will end with the strangest entry (that is, entry 63). The date of the marriage is uncertain because Wyatt noted that it was to be inserted at the '31st' of February 1739/40. In any event, it seems that Will Jones and Jennett Hunter went first to Burnford's marriage house to be married, but then appeared at Wheeler's. Wyatt noted that the bride dressed 'very fine', but looked like a 'common' woman who 'wanted' a man to personate. I believe that means that she dressed up to look like a man.

Folio 2 recto

1. Out of W: Wy
   Jan 1736/7. 19. Thomas PETT Gent Wye in Kent
   Mary FINMORE North Kensey Surry B S at Wheelers
2. 21. Thomas GARDINER Gent St James West*
   Ann CARSELEY B S 3 Tuns Tavern
   *[*Short for Westminster. The bride's place of residence is not noted]*
3. 30. Thomas MORRIS attorney at law
   Jane HALL B S Wilsons
   [The spouses' places of residence are not noted]
4. Feb 5th 1736/7. Isaac GAYNON Gent St James West
   Jane BEST Ditto B S Constables, Fleet lane
5. 7. Benjamin WILSON Allhallows Barkin upholsterer
   Elis. WEEBLE St Sepulchers *S at Kings Arms Tavern
   *[*The groom's condition is not noted]*
6. 7. Ambrose LAMBKIN Dimond Cutter St James
   Grace WATERMAN *S Wilsons
   *[*The groom's condition and the bride's place of residence are not noted]*
7. 7. David BEBAULT Surgeon St Clements Dean
   Mary GRAY Ditto B* Fighting Cocks
   *[*The bride's condition is not noted]*

Folio 3 verso

8. Out of W: W
   Feb. 1737/8 18th. Stephen CASALAR Linning* Draper St Anns Soho
   Elis. REGNIER B S at ye Bear Seacole Lane
   *[*Linen. The bride's place of residence is not noted]*
9. April 1738. 4. George REYNOLDS Gent St Peters in St Albans*
   Elis. MARSHALL W** Wilsons
   *[*In Hertfordshire. **The bride's condition and place of residence are not noted]*
10. 4. William GRIFFIN St Martins Silver Smith
    Mary LINSEY Ditto B W Wilsons
11. 6. Samuell JETTUR Gent Sart*
    *[*Short for servant. No details of the bride are noted]*
12. May 1738. 1. Phillip SIMMONDS Gent Sart* St Georges Hanover
    Ann BAXTER B W Hoop Tavern Fleet Market
    *[*Short for servant. The bride's place of residence is not noted]*
13. 1. Pastor Martin DUBLACK St Saviours
    Mary HIRAM B S Hoop Tavern Fleet Market
    [The bride's place of residence is not noted]
14. This taken for a memorandum
    Will THORNBOROUGHS Gent Northington in Southampton
    Ann DUGLAS* Mitcham in Surry W W
    *[*Presumably DOUGLAS. No specific date is noted for this entry, but the layout of the page suggests that the marriage could have been on the same date as the previous entry]*

Folio 4 recto

15. June 1738 Out of W: W
     5. Thomas JONES Gent St Andrews Houlborn
     Catherine JACOBS Ditto B S
     at Crooked Billet in which street behind St Clements church George Wheeler Clrk
16. 10. Sr. William MOORE Bart* St Andrews Holborn
     Sarah KING St Giles B S The 3 Tunn Tavern Snow Hill
     [*I have not been able to find this man in the standard reference works on
     baronets. He may have been lying about his status]
17. 22. Mathew MARTIN Gent Barnett*
     Ann JOHNSON Ditto B W at Wilsons
     [*In Hertfordshire]
18. 24. Silas VAWDREY Perukmaker St Lenoards Graicous Street
     Ann WEBSTER Aldersgate B S at Marshalls Fleet Market
     Dated Cert. 7th Novbr 1737*
     [*This is the first of the nine entries in this register in which it is stated that a
     backdated certificate has been provided or a backdated entry has been made in a
     marriage house register]
19. 27. John PETERSON Drawer St Pauls Covent Garden
     Ann GALE Ditto B S 3 Tunns Snow Hill
     Lawyer WILLMER TATHER* and gave her away
     [*I may have misread TATHER and so it is unclear whether WILLMER or TATHER is
     the lawyer's surname]
20. 29. John HUNT Gent St Pauls Covent Garden
     Mary NORMAND Ditto B S at Wheelers
21. 1738 July 6. John BEAMIS Gent St Georges Hanover
     Sarah PEDLEY Ditto W W at Laurances Rowbery* Fleet Lane
     [*This word is unclear]
22. 9. Thomas LITTLETON Gent St Martins in ye fields
     Franciscia Maria AUNGIOR Ditto B S at Marshalls Fleet Market
23. 15. Charles ANDERSON Gent St Pauls Shadwell
     Mary SPENCER Ditto B S at Burnfords

Folio 5 recto

24. July 1738 Out of W: W
     19. Edward GILBEC Gardiner Greenwhich*
     Ann KNIGHT B W Trydays Capt MACKPHEDRE present
     [*In Kent. The bride's place of residence is not noted. This entry is unusual in
     recording the presence of another person at the ceremony]
25. 21. Henry WEBB Gent St Georges Hanover
     Eliz WHEELER Ditto B S at Wilsons
26. 2?* Peter EDGERTON Gent St Georges Hanover Square
     Sarah HINES Ditto B S ye Butchers Armes
     [*Possibly 25]
27. 1738. Augt 8th Richard GRIMSTON Gent Greenwhich*
     Elinore CUNNINGHAM St James **S at Lilleys
     [*In Kent. **The groom's condition is not noted]
28. 8. MERRITT GEORGE marchants Clrk Aldermanbury
     Mary KYRK Ditto **S Woodwards
     [*It is possible that either GEORGE or MERRITT is the groom's surname. ** The
     groom's condition is not noted]

29.   12. Richard PARRY Grocier St Pauls Covent Garden
Hester TAPPEY* Ditto B W at Marshalls
[*This surname is unclear]

Folio 5 verso
30.   Augt 13th. Alexandr. SNAPE Brazier St Sepulchers
Sarah JORNEY Clarkenwell B W 3 Tunns Snow Hill
31.   14*. Jonathan JACKSON Gent Aldgate
Phobe WARREN Ditto W W
[*The date is unclear]
32.   18. Jeremiah LAMY Dimond Cutter St Bartholems.
Ann EVERTON Ditto B S at Broomhall ye Swann Ditch Side
Dated the Cert 25 Sept 1737

Folio 6 recto
33.   Out of W: W
Augt 31 1738. James CLEMENTS Gent St Edmonds the King Lumbard Street
Elisabeth TAYLOR St Pauls Covent Garden B S at Tarrells Bagnio, Long Acre
[This entry records a marriage outside the Fleet, at a bagnio near Covent Garden.
A bagnio was a bath house and often a brothel]
34.   Debr 21 1739. Hormon JOHNSON Gent St Giles in ye fields
Mary MEARLEY* St Giles B S at Last Shift
[*Possibly MCCARLEY]
35.   Sept 29* 1738. Robert SWARBRICK Gent St Georges Hanover Square
Mary MORAN St Mary Lebone B S Queens Head Grays Inn Lane
[*The date is unclear]
36.   1738 Sept 21. Wm. UMFREVILL Gent ye Inner Temple
Mary WELD St Mary WhitChapell B S
Mr. Ed UMFREVILL present performed at ye Temple
[William UMFREVILL was probably a barrister with chambers in the Inner
Temple]
37.   22 Sept 1738. Will MONROW Physician St Catherins
Sarah HALL Ditto W S Lillys
38.   24. James IRWIN Gent St James West
Mary EADNELL Ditto B S Dated Cert in 37
[An example of Wyatt providing a backdated certificate to the couple]
39.   Oct 3d 1738. John TIPPING St Gilles ye fields vintner
Eliz GOODMAN Ditto B S Anchor and Crown
40.   Oct 8 1738. James CLAYTON Gent City of Chichester in Sussex
Ann PARKER Ditto B S ye Fountain near St Sepulchres Church

Folio 6 verso
41.   Oct 1738. 23d. Edward MORGEN vintiner St Albans Wood Street
Margt JONES Ditto B S Lawrances Fleet Lane Rowabarge
42.   24. John CORK Farmer Hitchen in Hartfordshire
Sarah MARDELL Ditto B* at Crosiers
[*The bride's condition is not noted]
43.   25. David YEXLEY Goldsmith* &
Jane CAREY of Braintree in Essex Sp at Kings Head Boyces
[*The groom's place of residence and condition are not noted]

44. Novbr 1728 31. Stephen & Sarah at Lillys
   [No other details of the spouses are provided]
45. 7. Joseph PORTER Gent St Martins in ye fields
   Rachell KENNARD Ditto B S at Crosiers
46. 10. Thomas ROBERTS Cornfactor Dunstable*
   Sarah HUST** Ditto B W Wheelers turnagain Lane
   *[*In Bedfordshire. **This may be a mistake for HURST]*
47. 24. Tho. WHYTE Gent St Stephens Walbrook
   Martha WOOFATT Stoke Newington B W Fountain Tavern
48. Dbr. 1738. 11th. Samuell BURGOINE Gent. St James West
   Isabella MOUNTGOMREY Ditto B W Newmarket Alehouse
49. 20. George POSMORE Gent St Clements Dean
   Elis. BESFORD St Sepulchers B S Black Lyon Hosier Lane by Smithfield
50. 21. Will. COLLIER Farmer Hillington Midx
   Frances COLLIER Ditto W S at ye Swan Holbr. Bridge
51. 27. Whiston BRISTOW apothecary St Sepulchers
   Rebecca JACKSON B S Crown Fleet Market

Folio 7 recto
52. Decbr 1739*. 5. Peter CARRAFFE Gent St Georges Hanover
   Elis. PRICE Ditto B S at Bryces
   *[*The entries jump from December 1738 to December 1739]*
53. 9. William LINDEMAN Gent St Gregorys
   Mirram DAVIS Ditto B S Wilsons
54. 10. Will. COSTICK Gent St Mary in Kent
   Eliz. MANTON B S Wilsons
55. 10. John VERNON Gent St Clemons Dean
   Mary HODGSON St Dunstans in ye west B S Butcher Arms Fleet Market
56. 21. Harmon JOHNSON Gent St Giles in ye fields
   Mary MECARTEY Ditto B S Jack Last Shift Harp Alley
57. 25. James YOUNG Diamond Cutter St Antholins
   Elis MOORE Ditto B S Harlins
58. Jan 1739/40. 3d. Austin LEIGH Gent Xt Church Spile fields*
   Ann RICHARDSON Ditto B S Wilsons
   Dated Reg: Book at Wilsons June ??** 1739
   *[*Spitalfields. **The date in the month is illegible. A false date appears to have been given for this marriage in the register of Wilson's marriage house]*
59. 19. Daniel MACNEIL Gent St Mary Magd. Bermondsey
   Jane IVORY *S Barretts
   *[*The groom's condition and bride's place of residence are not noted]*

Folio 7 verso
60. Jan 1739/40. 19. Richard HART Gent Woolwich*
   Mary GEARY Ditto W W Boyces
   *[*In Kent]*
61. 26. John BASHAM Gent St James West
   Elis. FULLER Ditto B S Boyces
62. 27. Solomon & Jane at Lillys
   [No other details of the spouses are provided]

63. This to be inserted 31st* of Feb 1739/40 Will JONES vintiner of Covent garden B & Jennett HUNTER Ditto Sp at Wheelers they came first to Burnfords and would give but 5d she Drest very fine and looked like a common woman wanted a man to personate.
*[*See my note (Page 69) in the introduction to this register]*

64. Feb 1739/40. 4th. Will HARVEY Gent St Michaels Crooked Lane
Elis. BARFOOT Ditto B S Harlings

65. 5. Will CANN Gent St Martins in ye fields
Mary TURVEY GRUBB* Barhamstead Hartfordshire B** Biggs Fleet Lane
*[*GRUBB is probably the bride's surname but the names TURVEY and GRUBB are both indexed. **The bride's condition is not noted]*

66. 17. Richard REYNOLDS Clark Greenwhich*
Elis. PHILLPOT Ditto B S 3 Tunns Tavern
*[*In Kent]*

67. 17. Alexeander THAVANE Gent Cook St Ann Soho
Mary GOOLDING B S Jones
[The bride's place of residence is not noted]

68. 17. Aquilla DACKOMBE Gent St Martin
Jane WELLE B S Lands
[The bride's place of residence is not noted]

69. 21. Solomon SIMISON Gent St Georges Hanover
Elis. TUBB Ditto B* Bates Coffehouse Fleet Market
[The bride's condition is not noted]

70. March 3rd 1739/40. Joseph PEYTON Gent St Giles
Mary TAYLOR B S Lands dated cert Jan 25th 1738
[The bride's place of residence is not noted. This is another entry referring to the issue of a backdated marriage certificate]

71. 2d. Thomas CLARK Gent Allhallows Barkin
Mary YOUNG St Mary att Hill B S at 3 Tun Tavern Snow Hill
by the book nobody to see the book*
*[*Presumably a reminder that this marriage was to be kept secret]*

Folio 8 recto

72. March 1739/40. 9th. Christopher SMALL Gent Isleworth
Mary SMITH Ditto W W Stanly Fleet Lane

73. 18th. John MIERS locksmith St Giles
Elis PARTRIDGE Ditto B S
Dated crt Dbr 26th 1738 Says in ye Book in Newgate
[This marriage may have been recorded in a book at Newgate Prison. It does not appear in the register of Christ Church, Newgate Street (published by the Harleian Society)]

74. 20. Patrick DOLLARD Gent White Chapell
Mary LYON Ditto Boyces
[The spouses' conditions are not noted]

75. 1740. 7th April. Ralph CLAYTON Gent St Andrews Holborn
Elis. WILLBRAME St Clemonts Dean B S Boars Head Tavern, Cannon Street

76. 7. Thomas MANNING Gent Hanover Square
Dorothy WILEY Ditto W S Jones

77. 12. Robert HAMES Gent ye Erle of Pembrokes Regt
Mary STEED Watford* B W Lands
*[*In Hertfordshire]*

78. June 1740. 1* Edward ORPWOOD Vinctiner** Bishopgate
    Jane SNOW Ditto B W 3 Tunns Snowhill
    *[*The date is unclear. **Probably a mistake for vintner]*
79. 1*. John WAITE Gent Islington
    Joyce FLETCHER B S Wilsons
    *[*The date is unclear]*

Folio 9 recto
80. Jan 1738/9*. 2d. Richard JONES Vintiner St Dunstans in ye West
    Sarah MOYES Northmims B S Jack Last Shift Popin Court
    *[*The dates of the entries now revert to January 1738/9]*
81. 2d. James TAYLOR Vintiner Barnett Midx
    Catherine TRANTER Ditto B S ye Globe over against St Andrews church
82. 4. Saml. COCKS Gent of Hanover. I supose of Hanor. Square
    Rosamond FRIEND Ditto B S Boyces
83. 12. Lawrance RIGGS attorney at law St Bartholomews ye Less
    Margt PETTS St Clements Dean B W
84. 14. Stephen LARRU Goldsmith St Martin 'dont say which'
    Elis. SANDYS Ditto *S Datd. crt. 1st Aug 1738
    *[*The groom's condition is not noted. A further example of the issue of a
    backdated marriage certificate]*
85. 19. William ABERCRUMBIE Gent
    Jane YOULL St Martins B* S Jones
    *[*The groom's condition is unclear, but probably B, or bachelor, and his place of
    residence is not noted]*
86. Feb 1738/9. 5. John MAYNARD Gent St Anns Soho
    Martha TAYLOR Ditto B S dont say where*
    *[*This statement appears where the compiler of the register usually noted the
    place of the ceremony]*
87. 12. Henry POTTER Dimond Cutter Hackney
    Elis. GHISLIN or GISLIN* Ditto B S in fleet Lane (but Dont say what house)
    *[*Both surnames are given in the register]*
88. 10. Mathew WILLSON Gent St Dunstans
    Ann LEE St Pauls Covent Garden. B S Globe Hatton Garden Jon. Crosier Clrk.
89. 27. Richard WILLCOX Gent Barnett*
    Sarah MANN Ditto W** Sunn Coffe house Ditch Sides
    *[*In Hertfordshire. **The bride's condition is not noted]*
90. July 1st 1727. George COPETHORE* marriner Greenwhich**
    Elis. WOOD Deptford. B: W Entered in Fe. B S*** B: W or S
    *[*The groom's surname is unclear. **In Kent. ***This entry is very confusing. The
    groom seems to have been a bachelor, but it appears that Wyatt or the compiler of
    the register was unsure whether the bride was a spinster or widow]*

Folio 9 verso
91. March 1738/9. 5. Wm & Sarah mard. at Croziers. She kept the White horse Inn at
    Stains.
    [No other details of the conditions of the spouses are noted]
92. April 1739. 3d. Francis MULLET Cook to Lord Cavendish
    Mary ARCHER He a Frenchman. B S at hir one* house
    *[*This probably means at her own house The spouses' places of residence are not
    noted]*

93.   May 1739. 11. John HUMPHREYS Gent St Brids
        Mary HARVEY Covent Garden B W Boyces
94.   12. James RUTTER Gent St Giles in ye fields
        Jane WILLIAMS Ditto W S Broomhall
95.   31. Charles JONES Gent St Brides
        Hannah STEPPLE St Mathews* B S Sr John Falstaffs head Charing Cross
        [*Probably St Matthews Bethnal Green]
96.   June 1739. 3d. Wm. KEEN Gent Liberty of the Rolls
        Jane DENEGALL Ditto B S Willsons
97.   5. Thomas LOW Diamond Cutter St Sepulcher
        Rachel HELBERT B S Row Barge Fleet lane
98.   9. Michel GOODALE Surgeon St James
        Elis GEERING B*
        [*The bride's condition and place of residence are not noted. The place at which
        the ceremony took place is also omitted]
99.   10. John ROWLAND Bookseller St Mary Le Strand
        Elis TEARLEY St Martins B S Wheelers
100.   22. John BOWIE Gent St Martin
        Ann GRIFFITH B S Boyces
101.   30. John PITT Gent St Martin
        Elis. PEIRCE Ditto. B S 3 Tunns Snow hill. Matt Wilson Clrk.

Folio 10 recto

102.   July 1739. 7th. Marmeduke BIGNOLD Gent St Martin
        Rose MULLELY W W Woodward Sun Coffe house fleet Ditch
103.   Mistook one of ye 4th*. William TERWIN Gent St James West
        Mary TEMPLEMAN Raynah Essex W W Harlins
        dated crt 27th Novbr 1737
        [*This probably means that the entry is dated 4 July 1739, but the compiler only
        remembered to insert it after he had already written the above entry, of 7 July]
104.   8th. Wm RILEY Gent St James West
        Mary KINNION B*
        [*The bride's condition and place of residence are not noted. The place at which
        the ceremony took place is also omitted]
105.   8th. Thomas HALL Gent St James West
        Frances BROWN Ditto B S Halfmoon Tavern, Halfmoon street Strand
106.   17. Richard WILLS Gent St Georges Hanover
        Letitia BILLINGSLEY St Andrews Holborn B S
        Bellsaviage yard at ye Bellsaviage Inn
107.   28. Thomas STACK Gent St Andrews Houlborn
        Sarah MASON Ditto. B S Wheelers Reg* 3d. Sept 1738
        [*This probably means that the false date of 3 September 1738 was recorded in
        the register of Wheeler's marriage house]
108.   21. William ADKINS Papermaker High Wicomb in Bucks
        Mary FRANCIS Ditto B S at ye whors Inn* Fleet Ditch markett
        [*This is certainly the most interesting name that I have yet found for an Inn or
        marriage house. It may have been a name used locally for an inn, that had a more
        conventional name, but which was known as a brothel]
109.   21. Rodlph* STEINFELS Gent St James
        Nanny RITER W W Mrs Clark Turn again Lane
        [*Probably a mistake for Rudolph. The bride's place of residence is not noted]

110.   Oct 1739. 10. John ROW & Susanna* Wheelers
       *[*The bride's surname and the spouses' residence and conditions are omitted]*
111.   10. Wm. COKAYNE Gent Lambeth
       Margt CRAFFORD Ditto B W
       [The place at which the ceremony took place is not noted]

Folio 10 verso
112.   Oct 1739. 17. John COLLISON Gent Sunderland, County Durham
       Susanna HICKS B S Boyces
       [The bride's place of residence is not noted]
113.   19. Will DENIS Gent St Andrews Holbr.
       Martha DENNING Ditto B S Wilsons
114.   20. Robert RICHARDSON Gent St Clemonts Dean
       Elisabeth HICKS Ditto B S Boyces
115.   26. Will WOOD Surgeon White Chapell
       Barbara DEARGG Ditto W S Wilsons
116.   Novbr 4th. Thomas HURNALL Gent St Bartholomews Behind the Royal Exchange
       & Elisabeth KEEP Allhallows London wall B S
       at an apothecarys Behind the Royal Exchange*
       *[*In the City of London, some distance outside the Fleet]*
117.   9. John DAVIS Porter St Andrews*
       Mary NORTON Ditto W W Sands
       *[*Probably St Andrews Holborn]*
118.   9. John DAVIS Gent St Dionis Backchurch
       Elisabeth BELDUM W S ye new Market house
119.   12. John ELKANS Gent St Olives Hart Street
       Mary OLLFORD Ditto B S Lillys

End of the register in RG 7/163

Notebook of Marriages in piece RG 7/563

From 1726, September 1728 to December 1728 and January 1730

The notebook in piece RG 7/563 is described in the PRO class list as one of the notebooks of the minister John Floud, covering the Fleet marriages that he conducted from September 1728 to December 1728. This notebook is the only one that I can find that was used in the compilation of the register in piece RG 7/3. It is likely that other notebooks were also used, but they appear to have been lost or destroyed.

Most of the notebooks in the PRO collection (including this one) are of similar design and manufacture. They were intended as pocketbooks, to be carried on one's person so that notes could be made at any time. They were perfect for Fleet parsons who seem to have married people at any time of the day or night, and moved between different marriage houses, or even married people at their own homes. This notebook is about 5 inches by 3 inches, with a card cover of marbled design. It contains 46 paper folios. The PRO has stamped these as folios 1 to 46 and also stamped the inside rear cover as folio 47. The marriage entries commence on the inside cover. Folio 1 verso is blank and folio 1 recto is blank except for 'April 1726'.

A transcript of the notebook is set out below. The notebook does not include an index and the entries are not numbered and so, in this transcript, I have given numbers to each entry for ease of reference.

Illustration 6 is a copy of two pages from this notebook, folios 16 verso and 17 recto (entries 74 to 78 in the following transcript). The marriages are dated 8–10 October 1728. Each entry includes the name of the minister, John Floud, or his initials. As this is a notebook (or pocketbook) it is a reasonable assumption that these entries were written by Floud himself. They include one (entry 76), for the marriage of George Spurham and Elizabeth Creed, in which Floud records that he issued a backdated marriage certificate. In my opinion, most of the entries in the notebook are in this same handwriting. The exceptions are entries 1–3, 64, 67, 103, 108, 193 and 199–206. These are reviewed later in this introduction or in my notes to the transcript.

The notebook contains 205 entries of marriages and one entry for a baptism (entry 199). The PRO class list is correct in stating that the entries in the notebook cover the period September 1728 to December 1728. Entries 1–57, 65–194, 196–200 and 202–205 are from this period, but some entries are from other periods. Entries 58–64 are dated January 1730. Entry 195 is dated August 1726 and entry 201 is dated New Year's day 1726. The final entry in the notebook (entry 206) does not have a date but the marriage appears after entries of December

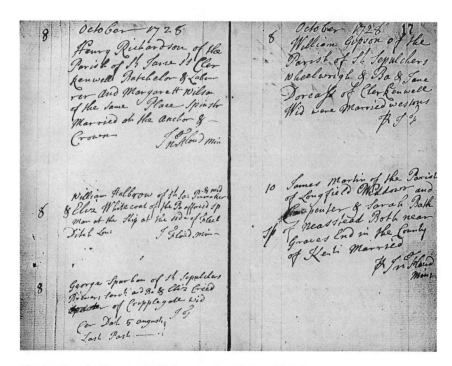

Illustration 6. Two pages(16 verso and folio 17) from the notebook in piece **RG 7/563**; marriages 8–10 October 1728

1728 and is stated to have taken place three years previously.

Most of the entries in the first half of this notebook (that is entries 1–63, 65–66, 68–100, 102 and 104–106) were copied into the register in RG 7/3. The entries in the second half of the notebook (that is entries 107–206) were not copied into the register (except for the marriages at entries 156–158, 178,180, 186, 198 and 204, and the baptism at entry 199). This copying is discussed further below.

Entries 1 and 129 may each record more than one marriage (see my notes to those entries). Furthermore, two of the marriages in the notebook each appear in two entries (see entries 23, 62, 67 and 103). Entry 23 records the marriage of William Hallin to Mary Swezland and it is repeated at entry 62. Both the entries are in Floud's handwriting. The first entry of this marriage (entry 23) appears between entries of September 1728, but Floud states that the ceremony was 'on what day of the month I cannot tell'. Entry 62 does not include a specific date for the marriage but it appears between two entries of 6 January 1730. It is impossible to say when this marriage took place.

The entry for the marriage of Benyamen Gilbeartson (or Gilbertson) and Elizabeth Willcox appears at both entries 67 and 103. At entry 67, it is undated but written between entries dated 7 October 1728. At entry 103 this same marriage is dated 28 October 1728. Both entries are in a different hand from that of John Floud and I suspect that the record of this marriage was inserted after most of the entries in the notebook. I cannot say why it was inserted twice. It is also impossible to say whether it is a true record of a marriage, or an entry inserted by a clerk in exchange for a payment from someone who wanted a record of such a marriage to exist.

Most of the entries are followed by the name John Floud, John Floyd or the initials 'JF', as the minister who conducted the ceremony. Some entries (such as entries 60 and 87) do not indicate the name of the officiating minister, but they are in the same handwriting as the Floud entries and were probably conducted by him. Three entries record marriages being conducted by other ministers. Entry 64 is in a different hand from that of Floud and is followed by the initials 'DW'. This is probably the Fleet parson Daniel Wigmore. This entry was not copied into the register in RG 7/3. It was either omitted by the clerk who copied the first half of the notebook, or was added into the notebook after that copying took place. Entries 108 and 204 are also not in Floud's hand. Entry 108 includes the name of the Fleet parson Ryder and entry 204 includes the initials 'JT' (probably John Tarrant, another Fleet parson). The baptism in this notebook (entry 199) is not in Floud's hand and it also includes the initials 'JT'. It was copied into the register in RG 7/3, where it includes (incorrectly) the name of Floud as the officiating minister.

John Floud, or Floyd as he often signed his name, performed thousands of marriages in the Fleet in the period 1709 to 1729. John Burn (in his work noted in the introduction to this volume) reported that Floud also married people at the King's Bench prison and in the Mint in 1725 and that he died suddenly, on 31 December 1729, at his lodgings in the Rules of the Fleet. Ashton (whose work is also referred to in the introduction) noted that the death occurred when Floud was conducting a wedding. Burn suggested that Floud was a man of bad character. The newspaper *The Post Boy*, of 8 January 1730, recorded that Floud was imprisoned for debt for several years and a Fleet register of 1727 reveals that Floud had a mistress by the name of Mrs Blood. Ashton notes that Floud sometimes used Greek to record entries or comments in his notebooks. He also recounts an interesting verse recorded by Floud in one of his notebooks:

I have liv'd so long I am weary of living,
I wish I was dead, and my sins forgiven;
Then I am sure to go to Heaven
Although I liv'd at sixes and sevens

The notebook contains many entries of special interest. I will refer only to some of these. The Fleet parsons sometimes included much more detail in their notebooks and registers than the Anglican parish clergy of the period. For example, entry 29 includes the occupation of the bride and entry 105 notes the bride's occupation and the place where she worked. Entry 83 gives the exact place of business of the groom. In entry 12, Floud records the name of the bride's village (and its distance from the nearest place of importance, Guildford in Surrey). Parish clergymen rarely noted such detail for the marriage of someone from outside their parish. The time of the marriage (10p.m.) is noted in entry 167. This was outside the canonical hours for marriages as noted in the introduction to this book.

The notebook also provides fascinating detail of the business of Fleet marriages. Entries 20 and 21 record the marriage of two couples in one ceremony (a fact not noted by the equivalent entries in the register in RG 7/3). Floud's wife assisted the marriage trade. In entries 55, 79 and 93, Floud notes that the couples were sent by his wife to Mrs Wilson's marriage house. Floud often recorded that he had provided a backdated marriage certificate to a couple. Notes to this effect appear in entries 4, 76, 90, 122, 159, 171, 184 and 195. The certificate might be backdated by a few months, but sometimes it was by a considerable period: seven years (entry 171), five years (entry 184) or four years (entry 195). In entry 25, Floud notes that the couple desired 'a setback', but he did not provide a certificate. Floud sometimes refused to provide a certificate (because the couple did not have enough money) and recorded his refusal, for example in entry 24 and in entry 71, where he wrote 'no certificate for want of money'.

In entry 52, Floud notes that he received six shillings for a marriage certificate and a licence. Like many Fleet parsons, he issued marriage licences without any valid ecclesiastical authority to do so. Entry 120 also refers to the couple having a marriage licence. However, the entry does not make clear whether this was a licence issued by an authorised official of the Church (which would not have granted permission for a marriage in the Fleet) or a licence issued by Floud.

The notebook records many of the taverns and marriage houses at which Floud and the other Fleet parsons plied their trade. Corbet's, Mrs Wilson's, the Vine, the Yorkshire Gray in Fleet Lane, Mr Balls, Burnford's, Mr Gilbert's, the Rainbow, the Shepherd and Goat, Clifton's and the Fighting Cocks are just some of the venues recorded in this notebook. Floud sometimes performed ceremonies at the spouses' own homes, or rooms. Entry 132 records a marriage at the couples' own room in St Giles and entry 171 records a ceremony being performed at the couples' own rooms at George Yard. Floud also performed ceremonies at his own house (see entry 13).

The Fleet parsons have been criticised since they began their trade. Much of this criticism is justified but some may be unfair. The parsons have been criticised for defects in their records of marriages, but at least they kept registers, sometimes of great detail. Some parish clergy of the eighteenth century failed to keep any record of the marriages, baptisms and burials that they conducted. Some defects in the Fleet Registers were not the fault of the parsons. Some people who were married in the Fleet were unwilling to provide full, or correct, information to Floud and his colleagues. Entry 91 in this notebook is a fascinating example. The notebook records the marriage of John and Martha, giving no surnames (and this entry was copied into the register in RG 7/3). However, this was not a case of a Fleet parson failing to record a marriage correctly. The entry in Floud's notebook records that the couple refused to give their full names. He noted his suspicion that this was a case of a gentleman marrying his maid. The couple refused to give their surnames despite Floud's request. They also refused to have a certificate and so Floud returned half their money. This suggests that Floud was not as dishonest or motivated by money as we might think. However, it would be going too far to suggest that the reputation of the Fleet parsons deserves a reassessment. The incident is recorded in the same notebook in which Floud recorded his unauthorised issue of marriage licences and his issue of certificates of marriage with false dates. The popular picture of Fleet parsons is probably justified.

The baptism (entry 199) and 110 of the marriages in the notebook (entries 1–63, 65–66, 68–100, 102, 104–106, 156–158, 178, 180, 186, 198 and 204) were copied into the register in RG 7/3 as the entries that I have numbered as 514–516, 518–605, 607–619, 651–653, 657, 670, 723 and 725 in the transcript of that register. They were copied with varying degrees of accuracy (as described in my introduction to that register). This confirms the importance of searching the notebooks, even though there are hundreds of them, for an entry of your ancestors' marriage already found in the registers. The notebook entries are likely to be more accurate than entries that were copied into registers. Even a small error in copying the name of one of the spouses could make it impossible for a researcher to find an ancestor's marriage in the register.

The clerk who copied the entries from this notebook into the register in RG 7/3 also omitted certain entries. As noted above, entry 64 is for a marriage conducted by Wigmore. This was not copied into the register in RG 7/3. Entries 67 and 103 from the notebook, for the marriage of Benyamen Gilbeartson (or Gilbertson) and Elizabeth Willcox, were also not copied into the register in RG 7/3. As noted, these were written into the notebook in a different hand from the other entries and it may be that they were only inserted after a clerk had copied the other entries into the register in RG 7/3. Entry 101 is in Floud's handwriting and seems to have simply been overlooked by the clerk who was preparing the register in RG 7/3.

We shall probably never know why only a few entries from the second half of the notebook appear in the register in RG 7/3. It may be that the others were only entered into the notebook after the other entries had been copied into the register. Or perhaps the copyist took a break after copying entry 106 into the register and then, for some reason, turned to another source, and only copied a few more entries from the notebook that interested him.

The register in RG 7/3 contains two entries, within the body of the entries that were copied from this notebook, that do not appear in the notebook. As noted in my introduction to RG 7/3 above, it is possible that John Floud had written those entries on scraps of paper which were perhaps loose in the notebook and which have now been lost.

The vast majority of people who were married in the Fleet came from London or those counties, such as Essex, Kent and Surrey, which were close to London. However, this notebook includes many people from other parts of Britain. Two couples came from Durham. Thomas Sweeting is recorded (in entry 2) as marrying Margaret Head (both were probably from Stockton). Entry 27 records a couple from Stanhope in Durham, George Lansdale and Margaret Curtis, marrying at the Castle in Old Bailey on 27 September 1728. On 25 October 1728, Henry Vaudery of Ashton upon Mersey in Cheshire married Anne Griffin from Towcester in Northamptonshire (entry 117). Richard Dimmery of Bristol married Jane Reason of Nottingham on 22 August 1726 and obtained a marriage certificate that was backdated to 1722 (entry 195). Mary Toplift of Plymouth married Richard Bridges of Chatham (serving on a naval ship) on 26 October 1728 (entry 121).

This notebook also illustrates the wide variety of classes and occupations of the people who married in the Fleet. 'Mariners' or 'sailors' appear in many entries; see for example entries 8, 50, 53, 90, 125 and 156. The man's ship is noted in entry 121, for the marriage of Richard Bridges of Chatham (serving on the Grafton man of war) and his bride Mary Toplift. There are also many soldiers, for example in entries 61, 71, 81, 95, 99 and 167. Their regiments are usually recorded, as in entry 61, for the marriage of John Hutchins of the 1st Regiment of Foot Guards and his bride Anna Maria Hall of St Martins in the Fields on 6 January 1730.

There are many farmers and husbandmen. Thus on 9 November 1728, William Francis, a husbandman of Wandsworth in Surrey married Elizabeth Taplis, also of Wandsworth (entry 154). Entries 108 and 169 record the marriages of gentlemen. Entries 123, 131 and 173 record the marriages of gentlemens' servants and entries 134, 135 and 176 record the marriages of labourers. Artisans and professionals also appear in the notebook. William Grace, a barber surgeon of Bishopsgate in the City of London married Mary Obbs (or Hobbs) on 20 November 1728 (entry 183). A merchant is recorded in entry 56, a tallow chandler at entry 34, glovers at entries 112 and 184 and cordwainers at entries 143 and 146.

Front cover verso

1.   Sept 1728. Geo and Francis and Anthony ELLIS at Coxes Warf ye Henry
        & Mary PINK
        *[No exact date is given for this entry. The handwriting (which is the same as that
        of entries 2, 3 and 199–206) is different to most of the entries in the notebook.
        The entries may have been added after most of the other entries. This entry may
        be a memo written by the minister, but it may record two or three marriages. The
        first part, naming George and Francis (with no surnames being given) has been
        copied, as entry 514, into the register in RG 7/3. The second part may be for a
        marriage of Anthony ELLIS, without his spouse being named. The third part may
        be a marriage of Henry and Mary PINK. If so, it is unclear whether PINK is the
        surname of the bride, or the surname of the groom (and therefore of the married
        couple). Another possibility is that this entry is only for one marriage – that of
        George and Frances (with no surnames being recorded, in the presence of three
        witnesses; Anthony ELLIS and a married couple, Henry and Mary PINK]*

2.   Thomas SWEETING & Margr HEAD Stockton of ye Brickburh Durham
        *[No exact date is given. See my note to entry 1 as to the handwriting of this entry.
        See entry 515 in the register in RG 7/3, which includes some copying errors,
        described in the note to that entry]*

3.   William TURNER & Jane BIGS of St Savours Southwark in Biurd Cage Walk*
        at Corbets
        *[*Bird Cage Walk. No exact date is given for this entry. See my note to entry 1 as
        to the handwriting of this entry. See also entry 516 in the register in RG 7/3,
        which includes some copying errors, described in the note to that entry. Following
        this entry, the register in RG 7/3 has an entry (that I have numbered 517) of 18
        September 1728, for the marriage of William ADDAMS and Mary CLIFFORD,
        which does not appear in this notebook]*

Folio 2 recto

4.   John BLACKBORN of the Parish of St Catherines By the Tower Mariner
        & Ruth HUTTON of the same place sp. Married at the Goat. The certificate dat. on
        the 11 of August but the cupple mar. on the 11 of October 1728
        *[An example of a notebook recording that a couple was provided with a backdated
        certificate (perhaps to predate the birth of a child). See also entry 518 in the
        register in RG 7/3, which includes some copying errors, described in the note to
        that entry. In that entry, the date is inexplicably noted as 18 September 1728]*

5.   19. James KEY of the Pa. of Christ church Surrey Ba and turner
        and Bethia SWETMAN of St Clements Dean Sp married 17 Day of may 1726
        according to the Rites and Ceremonies of the C of England as appears by this J
        Floud Min
        *[See entry 519 in the register in RG 7/3, which includes some copying errors,
        described in the note to that entry]*

Folio 2 verso

6.   Samuel ALLINGHAM of Betswerth near Rygate* widdow and Husbandman
        and Elliner HUTCHINS of the Pa. of Godlyman Spinster Mar: 16 Novr. 1728
        at Mrs Wilsons, Mr Jones came with them J F m
        *[*Probably Betchworth, near Reigate in Surrey. See entry 520 in the register in
        RG 7/3, which includes some copying errors, described in the note to that entry]*

Folio 3 recto
7.   Sep: 1728. 18. John READER of Bedworth Warwickshire brasier and wid
    & Mary WHITEHEAD of Islington widow at Picarings J F Min
[See entry 521 in the register in RG 7/3 which includes some copying errors, described in the note to that entry]
8.   18. John HOOD marriner & Ba
    and Mary HENFIELD Sp of the Citty of Wells* at Mr Westons w sheaf J F Min
[*In Somerset. See entry 522 in the register in RG 7/3 which includes some copying errors, described in the note to that entry]

Folio 3 verso
9.   19. Frances PARKINS of ye Pa. of Stoak in Buckinghamsh. Husbandman
    and Lydia RASH of the Pa. of Burnham Buckinghamsh. Ba & Sp. R bow
[See entry 523 in the register in RG 7/3 which includes some copying errors, described in the note to that entry and which has the initial 'F' for Floud which does not appear in this notebook. The note of R bow is a reference to the Rainbow Coffee House (or tavern), at the corner of Fleet Ditch, a famous marriage house]
10.   19. Joseph MARKS of the Pa of Aldgt* Bat & Spectaclemaker
    & Jonet CAMPBELL of ye same P. Spin: R Bow J F Min
[*An abbreviation for Aldgate. See entry 524 in the register in RG 7/3 which includes some copying errors, described in the note to that entry. For 'R Bow' see my note to entry 9 above]

Folio 4 recto
11.   1728. 20th. William MUNYON of St Sa* Ba & Mar
    and Anne MORGAN of the same P. Sp married at Picarings J F
[*Probably an abbreviation for St Saviours Southwark. See entry 525 in the register in RG 7/3 which includes some copying errors, described in the note to that entry]
12.   20. William WOOD of the Pa. of Godlyman Labourer and Ba
    & Anne PARRIS of the Pa. of Bamley 3 miles from Gilford* Mar. at Mother Wilsons J F Min. 4s No Certificate
[*Guildford in Surrey. See entry 526 in the register in RG 7/3]

Folio 4 verso
13.   21. William STONE of the Parish of Down near Cudham in Kent Ba & Husbandman
    and Anne PESCOTT of the Parish of Cudham Spinster Mar: at my House J F m
[See entry 527 in the register in RG 7/3 which includes some copying errors, described in the note to that entry. This is a rare entry recording that the marriage took place at the minister's own home]
14.   21. Robert WILLIAMS of Gravesend*
    and Eliz CANTRILL of Purfleet West Thurick Essex Mrs Wilsons
[*In Kent. See entry 528 in the register in RG 7/3 which includes some copying errors, described in the note to that entry]

Folio 5 recto
15.   22. Richard STANLEY of ye Pa. of St Buttolphs Bishops Gate Tayler & B
    and Jane JAMES of the Pa. of Lambeth Sp: Mar: R Bow John Floud
[See entry 529 in the register in RG 7/3 which includes some copying errors, described in the note to that entry. For 'R Bow' see my note to entry 9 above]

16.   23. Charles RICHARDSON
           and Amy WITNEY of Plishea near Chelmsford* at Burnfords Ba & Sp J F Min
           *[*In Essex. See entry 530 in the register in RG 7/3 which includes some copying
           errors, described in the note to that entry]*

Folio 5 verso
17.   23. Michael SIMPSON of ye Pa. of White Chappel Pipe ma. and Wid:
           and Jane DIXON of the Parish afforesaid Wid Mar R Bow J F
           *[See entry 531 in the register in RG 7/3 which includes some copying errors,
           described in the note to that entry. For 'R Bow' see my note to entry 9 above]*
18.   23. Edward ADDINGTON of ye Pa. of St James's Coachman and Ba
           and Jane BRADBERRY of the Pa. of St Georg's Hanover Square Spin: Mar R bow
           [See entry 532 in the register in RG 7/3. For 'R Bow' see my note to entry 9 above]

Folio 6 recto
19.   1728. 23. John ACHREMAN of ye Pa. of Aldgate Ba & wine cooper
           and Jane DAVIS of the Pa. of St John Wappin Spinster married at Mr Balls p. Jno
           Floyd Min
           *[See entry 533 in the register in RG 7/3, which includes some copying errors,
           described in the note to that entry]*
20.   23. John HARPER of the Pa. of St Georges Southwark Butcher and Batchelor &
           Marry CAREY of the Parish of Stepney Spinster mar at Balls JF
           *[See entry 534 in the register in RG 7/3, which includes some copying errors,
           described in the note to that entry]*
21.   Henry EMMERSON of the Pa. of Queenhith weaver & Ba
           and Anne SIMMONS of the Pa. of Coleman Street London at Mr Balls mar with one
           Cere two cuppll JF
           *[The marriage of two couples in one ceremony explains why it was not necessary
           for Floud to note the date for this entry. The entry runs on, without a gap, from the
           marriage of John HARPER and Marry (or Mary) CAREY, in entry 20. See also entry
           535 in the register in RG 7/3, which includes some copying errors, described in
           the note to that entry]*

Folio 6 verso
22.   24th Sep. Edward THOMPSON and Ann WAKER Ba and Sp:Both of Islington
           milkman mar at the Anchor & Crown JF Min
           [See entry 536 in the register in RG 7/3]
23.   William HALLIN of the Pa. of Strutham in Surry Ba
           &Mary SWEZLAND of the Parish of Croyden mar at the Castle and Magpy on what
           day of the month I cannot tell JF
           *[This entry is undated for the reason noted in the entry. It is repeated at entry 62
           below. See also entry 537 in the register in RG 7/3, which includes some copying
           errors, described in the note to that entry. See also entry 576 in RG 7/3]*
24.   24. Humphry GRAPE of the Pa. of Shoreditch Framework Knitter & Ba
           and Eliz ORAM of the same place Spinster mar at Ms Wilsons Noe certificate for
           less than 2 shill. JF
           *[The couple seem to have been refused a certificate of their marriage due to their
           limited means. See entry 538 in the register in RG 7/3, which includes some
           copying errors, described in the note to that entry]*

Folio 7 recto

25.   24. William THOMARVER Sawyer of the Pa. of Thorp
and Jane WAKEFORD of ye Pa. of Woking* Ba & Sp No certificate.
Desird a Setback
[*In Surrey. See entry 539 in the register in RG 7/3 which includes some copying errors, described in the note to that entry. The groom's surname in this entry is difficult to read and is written above the gap between 'William' and 'Sawyer'. It appears to have been missed by the clerk who was copying entries into the register in RG 7/3 (and so he named the groom as William SAWYER)]

26.   25. James WOOD of the Pa. of St Clements Dean Ba & Fruterer
& Anne WILLSON of the Pa. afforesaid Sp
at the Blacklyon in Stonecutters Street JF M
[See entry 540 in the register in RG 7/3]

Folio 7 verso

27.   Sep 27. George LANSDALE of the Parish of Stanhope in ye Bishoprick of Durham*
now in Long Lane near White Street near the Green Man & Artichoak in the Pa of St Mary Magdalenes and Margaret CURTIS of the Pa. and same place afforesaid Wid mar at the Castle in the Old Bayley JF
[*At this point, the following words have been written, but then crossed out 'Lives now in Whites Street near St Georges Church Southwark'. See entry 541 in the register in RG 7/3]

28.   28. John LEVERIDG of the Pa. of St Bennetts Pauls Wharf Chairmaker and Ba
and Febe BOZE of the same place Spinster Mar at the Yorkshire Gray Fleet Lane
[See entry 542 in the register in RG 7/3]

29.   Sep 28. James WARD of the Pa. of Stepney Marriner & Ba
and Hannah UNDERWOOD of the Pa. of St James's Clerkenwell wid & hatmaker at Mr Ball JF
[See entry 543 in the register in RG 7/3]

Folio 8 recto

30.   29. John ELLIS of Shoreditch
and Anne REICH of the same at Picaringds Stockinframework knitter JF
[See entry 544 in the register in RG 7/3, which includes some copying errors, described in the note to that entry]

31.   29. Rowland KING of Bexley in Kent Husbandman & Ba
& Mary WILLIAMS of the same Sp at Mrs Wilsons JF M
[See entry 545 in the register in RG 7/3]

32.   29. Mathew LEE of the Pa. of White chapple weaver & Ba
and Anne FRANKLIN of the same Sp and weaver R. Bow J F
[For 'R Bow' see my note to entry 9 above. See also entry 546 in the register in RG 7/3]

33.   29. John ROFEER* of St Maryhill Ba
and Eliz MURFIT of St Ollive Surry Wid mar JF M
[*Possibly ROTEER. See also entry 547 in the register in RG 7/3]

Folio 8 verso

34.   29. Thomas LUCAS of the Parish of St Margarets Westminster tallow chandler and of the Colestream Regiment of Guards Br of Scarborough of Folliott company and Margaret STEPHENS of MaryLebone mar at the Anchor & Crown J Floyd Min
[See entry 548 in the register in RG 7/3, which includes some copying errors, described in the note to that entry]

35.   29. Miles CONNER of the Pa. of Enfield Ba & husbandman
& Hannah LAMBERT of the Pa. of St Martins Ludgate widdow married at Mr Balls J Floyd Min
[See entry 549 in the register in RG 7/3]

Folio 9 recto

36.   29. Thomas MATTOCKS of the Pa. of St Andrews Holborn Farrier & Batchelor
& Hannah DENT of the Pa. of ye same place Sp Mar. at the Bores head Stonecutters Street
[See entry 550 in the register in RG 7/3]

37.   30. Edward SAUNDERS of the Pa. of Covent Garden Ba & Vintner
& Mary HEALE of the Pa. of St Andrews Holborn Wid & Mar. at R Bow JF Min
[For 'R Bow' see my note to entry 9 above. See also entry 551 in the register in RG 7/3, which includes some copying errors, described in the note to that entry]

Folio 9 verso

38.   30. Henry HAYDON of the Pa. of East Tilberry in the County of Essex husbandman Ba and Lydia BYFORD of ye same Place Spinstr R Bow JF
[For 'R Bow' see my note to entry 9 above. See also entry 552 in the register in RG 7/3]

39.   30. Robert GODDARD of the Pa. of St Saviours wid & Potter
& Barbary WHARTON of the Pa. of the same Sp at the Wheat Sheaf JF M
[See entry 553 in the register in RG 7/3 which includes some copying errors, described in the note to that entry]

40.   30 Richard MARTIN of the Pa. of Darn in the County of Kent two miles from Dartford Bachelor and husbandman
and Sarah WILLDAM of the Pa. of Willminton Spinster Mar at the Castle in Old Bayley J Floud Min
[See entry 554 in the register in RG 7/3]

Folio 10 recto

41.   30. Richard JONES of Bosleham in Staffordshire Turner & Ba
and Anne LEE of the Pa. of Hazlemore in the County of Surry Wid at the Castle and Magpy J F Min
[See entry 555 in the register in RG 7/3]

42.   30. Andrew GOSHAM the Pa. of St Anns Black Fryers Snuff Boxmaker
and Mary JONES of the Pa. of Folston* in the County of Kent seven miles from Dover Sp Mar at Nat Janes's p Jno Floyd Min
[*Probably Folkestone. See entry 556 in the register in RG 7/3, which refers to Folkston]

Folio 10 verso

43.   Oc 1 1728. John BROOKS of the Pa. of Brogsdon Hartford Husbandman and Ba
Mary LYNSEY of the same Sp R bow JF
*[For 'R bow' see my note to entry 9 above. See also entry 557 in the register in RG
7/3, which includes some copying errors, described in the note to that entry]*

44.   2. Thomas COLLIN of the Pa. of West Malling in Kent Gardner & Ba
& Mary TONG of the same Sp Ra Bo*
*[For 'Ra Bo' see my note to entry 9 above. See also entry 558 in the register in RG
7/3, which includes some copying errors, described in the note to that entry]*

45.   2. John JUDD of the Parish of Yoldin in Kent Husbandman and Ba
& Eliz BENNETT of the Pa. of Huntton Sp Mar R Bow
*[For 'R Bow' see my note to entry 9 above. See also entry 559 in the register in RG
7/3, which includes some copying errors, described in the note to that entry]*

Folio 11 recto

46.   2. Thomas SANDERS of the Pa. of Walton of the Hill Husbandman and Ba
and Mary RICHARDSON of the same place Spinster Jno Floud
*[See also entry 560 in the register in RG 7/3, which includes some copying
errors, described in the note to that entry]*

47.   2. William STILES of the Pa. of Rootham in the County of Kent Husbandman and
Batchelor and Margaret HOW of same place Sp at Mr Jones's at*
St Georges Church J Floyd Min
*[*Probably a mistake for 'near'. See also entry 561 in the register in RG 7/3,
which includes some copying errors, described in the note to that entry]*

Folio 11 verso

48.   2. William WALL of the Pa. South Frambridge in Rotchford Hundred Essex yeoman
& Mary SMITH of the same Mar. at Mr Sedgwicks in Long Lane
Cer: Dat Whitson Tuesday JF Min
*[An entry that records the backdating of a certificate. See entry 562 in the
register in RG 7/3, which has been dated incorrectly as 3 October and which
includes some other copying errors, described in the note to that entry]*

49.   3. Thomas PEWTRIS of Berkin in Essex & Mary KELSHEW of Burnstead* near
Brantery** in Essex Maried Ba & Sp at the Anchor and Crown JF
*[*Possibly Bumstead. **Presumably Braintree. See entry 563 in the register in
RG 7/3, which includes some copying errors, described in the note to that entry]*

Folio 12 recto

50.   3. Francis HAYLOCK of the Pa. of Tisberry in Wiltsh. Ba a Marriner
& Eliz HOOPPER of the Pa. of Deptford in the County of Kent Married R bow p. J
Floyd Min
*[For 'R Bow' see my note to entry 9 above. See also entry 564 in the register in RG
7/3, which includes some copying errors, described in the note to that entry]*

51.   3. Thomas BURLIN of the Pa. of Stafford* Carpenter Ba
and Mary STANES of the Pa. of Barkin Spinster Mar at ye R Bow
*[*This may be Stafford in Staffordshire, but is more likely to be the parish of
Stratford in Essex. For 'R Bow' see my note to entry 9 above. See also entry 565 in
the register in RG 7/3, which includes some copying errors, described in the note
to that entry]*

Folio 12 verso

52.   3 October 1728. Johnnathan LAUGHLIN of the Pa. of Lee in the County of Essex*
        Husbandman & Batchelor and Eliz FREEMAN of the Parish afforesaid Sp
        Mar Lycence certificate 6s. JF Min.
        *[*Probably a mistake for Kent. See entry 566 in the register in RG 7/3]*

53.   Octo 4th 1728. Ezekiah OGLE of the Parish of Stepney Seafaringman
        and Mary GARDNER of the same place Ba & Widdow R Bow JF 9 – 6*
        *[For 'R Bow' see my note to entry 9 above. *The '9 – 6', noted in the margin, is
        probably the fee of 9 shillings and sixpence. See also entry 567 in the register in
        RG 7/3]*

54.   4. John WAKLIN of the Parish of Southfleet Husbandman & Batchelor
        & Mary BATES of the Pa. afforesaid Sp R Bow J Floud M 7 – 6*
        *[For 'R Bow' see my note to entry 9 above. *The '7 – 6', noted in the margin, is
        probably the fee of 7 shillings and sixpence. See also entry 568 in the register in
        RG 7/3, which includes some copying errors, described in the note to that entry]*

Folio 13 recto

55.   Octo: 3 1728. Thomas MILES of the Pa. of Wappin Stepney Marriner and
        Coleheaver & Eliz BASFOOT of the same place Sp sent by my wife to Mrs Wilsons
        JF Min 9 spent 4s fee
        *[Mrs Floyd assists her husband's business. See also entry 569 in the register in
        RG 7/3, which includes some copying errors, described in the note to that entry,
        and the date is incorrectly noted as 4 October]*

56.   5. John NUTS of St Giles' in ye Field merchant
        & Jane DEAKERS of ye same at Mr Balls Jno Floud Private*
        *[*The word private is written in the margin. See also entry 570 in the register in
        RG 7/3 which includes some copying errors, described in the note to that entry]*

57.   6. Richard DUNMAR of the Pa. of Christ Church soutw* Labourer and widdow and
        Susanna SWERET of the same place Mar at Wilsons JF
        *[*Soutw is presumably short for Southwark. The bride's surname is difficult to
        read, but is probably SWERET. See also entry 571 in the register in RG 7/3,
        which also has SWERET as the bride's surname, but includes some copying
        errors, described in the note to that entry]*

Folio 13 verso

58.   Jany 6 1730. William GRAVET of Mecham* in Surry Husbandman and wid
        and Margaret REED of the same place Mar at Mrs Wilsons JF
        *[*Probably Mitcham. See entry 572 in the register in RG 7/3, where this entry
        and those following (up to entry 64) have been incorrectly dated 6 October 1728.
        All the entries on folios 13 verso and 14 recto of this notebook are actually dated
        6 January 1730, whereas most of them have been copied into the register in RG
        7/3 as 6 October 1728. Marriages of 6 October 1728 then carry on at folio 14
        verso (entry 65) of the notebook. These marriages of 1730 may appear between
        marriages of 1730 because Floud was been using two blank pages in his
        notebook that he had omitted to use in 1728. It may be that the clerk copying the
        entries into RG 7/3 did not notice the sudden change in dates, since the entries
        before and after these of 1730 were all of the sixth of the month]*

59.   6. William GRAY of the Pa. of St Dunstane Stepney or Wappin Stepney wido
        and Isabella HARDOM of the same place Spinster Mar at Picarings JF M
        *[See entry 573 in the register in RG 7/3, which includes some copying errors,
        described in the note to that entry. See also the note on dates at entry 58 above]*

60.   6. Edward HIVE of the Parish of Shadwell Ba & Seafaringman
         and Eliz ATKINS of the same wid at R bow
         *[See entry 574 in the register in RG 7/3 and the note on dates at entry 58 above.
         For 'R bow' see my note to entry 9 above]*

Folio 14 recto

61.   Jan 1730. 6. John HUTCHINS of the first R. of Guards Ba and Anna Maria HALL
         of St Martins in the Field Wid Maried at Mrs Willsons J Floud minr.
         [See entry 575 in the register in RG 7/3 and the note on dates at entry 58 above]
62.   William HALLIN Strutham* Batchelor
         and Mary SWEZLAND both of Croydon Mar at the Cas Old Bayley
         *[*In Surrey. No date is specified for this entry, which repeats entry 23 above (in
         which Floud stated that he did not know the date). See also entry 576 (and entry
         537) in the register in RG 7/3 and the note on dates at entry 58 above]*
63.   6. Richard BARTON of the Pa. of St Andrews Holborn Ba and Butcher
         and Eliner MIARS of the Pa. of St Clements Dean at Westons JF
         *[See entry 577 in the register in RG 7/3 which includes some copying errors,
         described in the note to that entry. See also the note on dates at entry 58 above]*
64.   6. John KITCHNER of wtfryers & Ruth MASON of Do. DW
         *[See the note on dates at entry 58 above. However, this entry was not copied into
         the register in RG 7/3. It is in a different hand from other entries in this notebook
         and the officiating minister is noted as DW (probably Daniel Wigmore). This
         entry may have been omitted by the clerk who was copying entries into RG 7/3
         because it was not conducted by Floud. Alternatively, it may be that the entry was
         only inserted in this notebook after the copying into RG 7/3 had taken place]*

Folio 14 verso

65.   Octo 6 1728 William HINKLEY of the Pa. of Mecham*
         and Mary FRANCIS sp of the same place Married JF M
         *[*Probably Mitcham in Surrey. The dates in this notebook now revert to October
         1728. See also entry 578 in the register in RG 7/3]*
66.   7. Wm HAMMOND of the Pa. of Shoram in Kent Husbandman & Batchelor
         & Jane LATTER of the Pa. of Otford in Kent Spinster Mar: pr J Flod Min
         *[See entry 579 in the register in RG 7/3, which includes some copying errors,
         described in the note to that entry]*
67.   *Benyamen GILBEARTSON woolcomber of the Parish of Styton widower
         and Elizabeth WILLCOX of ye same Do. Spinster
         *[*This entry has no date and is in a very different hand from most of the entries in
         this notebook. It also appears at entry 103 below, but was not copied into the
         register in RG 7/3. It was probably inserted later]*

Folio 15 recto

68.   7 of Octo 1728. Sammuel BENNET of St Andrews Holborn wid
         Susanna DARBY of St Giles's in the Fields Sp at Picaring J Floud min
         [See entry 580 in the register in RG 7/3]
69.   7. Tho: BIRD of the Pa. of Ainsford near Farningham Husbandman & Ba
         & Mary ALTRIP of the Pa. of Shoram Sp R Bow JF
         *[For 'R Bow' see my note to entry 9 above. See also entry 581 in the register in RG
         7/3]*

Folio 15 verso

70.   Octo 7 1728. Robt. SMALL of the Parish of St Sepulchers London Spectaclemaker and Sarah MAYHEW of the Pa. of Blackfryers Spinster Willsons J* Min
*[*Only the initial J appears, instead of JF. See also entry 582 in the register in RG 7/3, which includes some copying errors, described in the note to that entry]*

71.   7. George BRITEWELL of the First Re. Of Guards Sol. & Ba & Margaret BELL of the Pa. of St Martins in the Fields Spinster Mar. Jno Floyd Min. No Cert. For want of money
[The couple seem to have been refused a certificate of their marriage due to their limited means. See entry 583 in the register in RG 7/3, which includes some copying errors, described in the note to that entry]

Folio 16 recto

72.   1728. 8. Edward EDWARDS of the Pa. Devis's Wiltshire Ba. & wid and Eliz CANNING St Gabriel Fanchurch Street London J* Cliftons
*[*Only the initial J appears instead of JF. See also entry 584 in the register in RG 7/3. Following this entry in the register in RG 7/3, there appears (as entry 585) a baptism dated 8 October 1728 of Wm. SMITH son of John & Ann SMITH. This entry appears later in this notebook, on folio 46 recto (see entry 199 below and my notes to that entry)]*

73.   8. Tobias GOBART of the Pa. of St Martins in the Field Ba and Taylor & Mary CAWOOD of the Pa. of St Martins afforesd. Spinstr R Bow JF
[For 'R Bow' see my note to entry 9 above. See also entry 586 in the register in RG 7/3]

Folio 16 verso

74.   8 October 1728.Henry RICHARDSON of the Parish of St James's Clerkenwell Batchelor & Labourer and Margarett WILSON of the same place Spinstr. Married at the Anchor & Crown Jno Floud Min
[See entry 587 in the register in RG 7/3]

75.   8. William HALBROW of St Sa* Pinmaker & wid & Eliz WHITECOAT of the Pa. afforesd Sp Mar at the Ship at the side of Fleet Ditch Lon: J Floud Min
*[*Probably short for St Saviours. See entry 588 in the register in RG 7/3, which includes some copying errors, described in the note to that entry]*

76.   8. George SPURHAM of St Sepulchers Brewers Servt. and Ba & Eliz CREED of Cripplegate wid JF Cer Dat. 5 August last past
[Another specific reference by Floud to his backdating of certificates. See also entry 589 in the register in RG 7/3]

Folio 17 recto

77.   8 October 1728. William GIPSON of the Parish of St Sepulchers Wheelwright & Ba & Jane DORCASS of Clerkenwell Wid were married Westons p. JF
[See entry 590 in the register in RG 7/3, which includes some copying errors, described in the note to that entry]

78.   10. James MARTIN of the Parish of Longfield Widdower and Carpenter & Sarah BATH Sp of Neasstead both near Graves End in the County of Kent Married p. Jno Floud Min
[See entry 591 in the register in RG 7/3, which includes some copying errors, described in the note to that entry]

Folio 17 verso

79.   11 October 1728. John HOSGOOD of the Pa. of Crediton* Clothier and Ba
        and Anne SHAW of the Pa. of Alhallow Berkin near the Tower widdow
        married at Mrs Wilsons, sent by my wf. J Floyd Min
        *[*Presumably Crediton in Devon. Mrs Floyd assists her husband's business, as in
        entry 55. See also entry 592 in the register in RG 7/3, which includes some
        copying errors, described in the note to that entry]*

80.   12. George WORRIL of the Pa. of Stepney Ba & Labourrer
        and Elizth. STRATFORD of the Pa. of Newington Butts sp Mar at Mrs Wilsons JF M
        *[See entry 593 in the register in RG 7/3, which includes some copying errors,
        described in the note to that entry]*

Folio 18 recto

81.   12. Arthur BULMAN of My Ld. Mycarrs marching Regiment of foot Married at ye R
        Bow and Mary EARLE of the Pa. of St Lawrence's Redding* JF Min
        *[For 'R Bow' see my note to entry 9 above. *One of the three ancient parish
        churches of Reading in Berkshire. See also entry 594 in the register in RG 7/3,
        which includes some copying errors, described in the note to that entry]*

82.   12. Henry SCOMB* of the Pa. of Stepney Weaver Ba
        and Ruth ASHLEY of the same sp. Mar R bow JF M
        *[*Probably the minister's spelling of SECOMB. See also entry 595 in the register
        in RG 7/3, which includes some copying errors, described in the note to that
        entry. For 'R bow' see my note to entry 9 above]*

83.   12. George COX of Bishopsgate Street Cornchandler & Ba at the New Signe of the
        sun at the End of Lamd Ally and Hester UFFORD of Shores Ditch Sp at the Fighting
        cock JF Min
        [See entry 596 in the register in RG 7/3]

Folio 18 verso

84.   Octo 13 1728. Thomas WATERS of the Pa. St Pauls Covent Garden Wid
        and Mary FOSTER the Pa. of St James Westminster Cliftons JF Min
        *[See entry 597 in the register in RG 7/3, which includes some copying errors,
        described in the note to that entry]*

85.   13. John BURN of the Pa. of St Catherine by ye Tower
        and Mary HADDERWICK of the same place Spinster Mar R Bow JF
        *[For 'R Bow' see my note to entry 9 above. See also entry 598 in the register in RG
        7/3, which includes some copying errors, described in the note to that entry]*

Folio 19 recto

86.   1728. 13. Thomas FIRTH of the Pa. of Shoreditch Hostler and Ba
        & Margaret ROBETSON of the same place Spin Mar at the Ship Ditch side JF
        *[See entry 599 in the register in RG 7/3, where the bride's surname is noted
        (probably correctly) as ROBERTSON]*

87.   13. Robert CROWDIRS of the Pa. of Queenhith and Hannah BENTLEY of the Pa.
        of St Sepulchers Ba & Spinster at the Red Lyon Ditchside
        [See entry 600 in the register in RG 7/3]

Folio 19 verso

88.   14 Octo 1728. Danniel DAVIS of the Parish of Lowlayton Ba and Labourer
        and Eliz: PERRING of Low Layton sp Mar R Bow JF
        *[For 'R Bow' see my note to entry 9 above. See also entry 601 in the register in RG
        7/3]*

89.   14. John ROWSE of the Parish of Finchley Labourer* ??dman and Ba
        and Mary SHAW of the Parish of Deptford both in the County of Kent Spinster
        Rain Bow Jno Floud Min
        *[*The word labourer has been crossed out and another occupation for the groom
        written underneath; unfortunately it is unclear. It may be 'Hsdman' (that is
        husbandman). For 'R Bow' see my note to entry 9 above. See also entry 602 in the
        register in RG 7/3 which includes some copying errors, described in the note to
        that entry]*

Folio 20 recto

90.   1728. 14. John GROSS of the Pa. of Stepney in Lymehouse Seafaringman
        and Mary GILLAM of Limehouse Wid Married 2s 1728 R Bow
        Cer to bare Date 22 August 1727
        *[For 'R Bow' see my note to entry 9 above. Another specific reference by Floud to
        his backdating of certificates. See also entry 603 in the register in RG 7/3, which
        includes some copying errors, described in the note to that entry]*

91.   14. John & Martha no certificate. Married at Mr Balls but no other names could be
        got from them, a Gent mar: I suppose his maid Refusd to have a Certificat at any
        Rate pd a Guiny. I Returnd 1/2 a Guiny
        *[A fascinating entry, discussed in the introduction above. See also entry 604 in
        the register in RG 7/3]*

Folio 20 verso

92.   1728. 14. Matthew WALKER of the Parish of St George the Martyr Weaver and Ba
        and Sarah SAVAGE the Parish of St Saviours Southwark J Floyd Min
        *[See entry 605 in the register in RG 7/3. That entry is followed by an entry (that I
        have numbered 606) that was not copied from this notebook]*

93.   15. Thomas LARK of the Parish of St Mary Whitechappel Batchelor
        & Elliner GARDNER of the Pa. afforesd Wid:
        sent by my wife to Mrs Wilsons J Floud Min
        *[Mrs Floyd assists her husband's business, as in entries 55 and 79. See also entry
        607 in the register in RG 7/3]*

Folio 21 recto

94.   15th. James LAWALLEY of the Pa. of St Pauls covent Garden Chairman and
        Batchelor & Elliner WENTWORTH of the Parish afforesaid Sp married at the Barly
        Mow and Magpy Fleet Lane J Floud Min
        *[See entry 608 in the register in RG 7/3, where the groom is incorrectly named
        John rather than James]*

95.   15. John JOHNSON of the 2 Regiment of Guard Soldier and Batchelor
        and Mary SMITH of the Parish of Aldgate Spinster
        Mar in Bell Savage Yard Ludgate Hill Mary Woodalls House J F min
        [See entry 609 in the register in RG 7/3]

Folio 21 verso

96. 1728. 15. Samuel BECH of the Parish of Cripplegate Batchelor
and Mary DEMAN of the same place Spinster Married at the Barly Mow and Magpy
Fleet Lane J F
[See entry 610 in the register in RG 7/3]

97. 17. Henry FLOUDGATE of the Parish of St Georges Southwark Cordwainer and
Widdow and Mary BARNS of St Mary White Chapple Wid Mar R Bow J Floud Min
[For 'R Bow' see my note to entry 9 above. See entry 611 in the register in RG 7/3]

98. 17. William TAYLOR of St Andrews Holborn Carpenter & Batchelor
and Sarah REDHEAD of Stepney Spinster at Balls JF M
[See entry 612 in the register in RG 7/3]

Folio 22 recto

99. 18*. Edward HOLMES of St Tockmans in Derby & of Brigadeer Kirks Re. Of foot &
Ba and Eliz WHITE of St Giles's Sp: Mar at the Anchor & Crown J Floud Min
*[*Altered from 17 to 18. See also entry 613 in the register in RG 7/3, where the
date is given as 17. It may be that the copying into RG 7/3 was undertaken before
the date was changed]*

100. 18*. Wm COLEY of the Pa. of St Giles's Cripple: Gate Carpenter and Batchelor
and Hannah BAGLEY of the Parish of Aldergate at the Fighting cocks JF Min
*[*Altered from 17 to 18. See also entry 614 in the register in RG 7/3, where the
date is given as 17. It may be that the copying into RG 7/3 was undertaken before
the date was changed]*

Folio 22 verso

101. October 19 1728. Robert LUCAS of the Parish of Bloomsberry Seafaringman & Ba
and Sarah CHAMBERS of the Parish of Stoak in Hampshire Widdow Mar: R Bow J
Floyd Min
*[For 'R Bow' see my note to entry 9 above. This entry was not copied into the
register in RG 7/3. It is in the same handwriting as most of the entries in this
notebook and does not seem to have been inserted later, so it is likely that the
clerk preparing the register in RG 7/3 simply omitted to include it]*

102. Octo: 20 1728. John DAVIS of the Pa. of Stepney Marriner & Ba
and Eliz MASON of the same place Spinster R B J F
*[For 'R B' see my note to entry 9 above. See also entry 615 in the register in RG
7/3]*

103. 28. Benyamen gilbear* GILBERTSON woolcomber of ye Parish of Styton widower
and Elizabeth WILLCOX of ye same Do. Spinster
*[*The minister started to write the groom's surname and then wrote the whole
surname without crossing out his incomplete attempt. This entry also appears at
entry 67 above. It is in a very different hand from most of the entries in this
notebook and it was not copied into the register in RG 7/3]*

Folio 23 recto

104. Octo 20 1728. Thomas CHRISWELL of the Parish of St Mary Maudlin Bermundsey
and Anne BULY of the same place Sp: JF Min
*[See entry 616 in the register in RG 7/3, which includes some copying errors,
described in the note to that entry]*

105.   20. Thomas WILLIAMS of ye Pa. of Clerkenwell Glasspolliser or woolcomer and
         wid and Jane SMITH of the Pa. of Clerkenwell wid and Churing woman at Ailsbury
         Street at a Cornchandlers near ye Stonecutters arms Jno Floud min
         [See entry 617 in the register in RG 7/3. A rare example of the bride's occupation
         (and her place of work) being noted]

Folio 23 verso

106.   1740 May 20. James REVE of Pitsey*
         and Martha WARNER of South Bently* wid & wid Rain low
         [*The spouses' places of residence are probably Pitsea and South Benfleet in
         Essex. For 'Rain low' see my note to entry 9 above. This entry has been copied into
         the register in RG 7/3 at entry 618 (but with the date 21 October 1728). Folios
         23 verso and 24 recto of this notebook (entries 106 to 110) have the dates 20
         and 22, so seem to carry on from the previous entries, but 'May 1740' has been
         written on each page. The entries on folios 24 verso and 25 recto have dates of
         22, 23 and 24, so seem to carry on in sequence (but the month and year are not
         stated). The entries on folios 25 verso and 26 recto have dates of 24 and 25, so
         also seem to carry on in sequence (but are marked 1728). The remainder of the
         entries in the notebook (apart from a few insertions) seem to be from November
         and December 1728, so I suspect that the 'May 1740' on folio 23 verso does not
         relate to the entries and that they are really from 20 and 22 October 1728]
107.   20. Edward GARLAND of Stepney Sailmaker and Batchelor
         and Eliz UMBER wid of the same mar at Mr Balls JF
108.   20. Edward COMSON* Gent Widower and Marey YOUNGER Spr Ryder
         [*This name is unclear. This entry is in a different hand from most of the entries
         in the notebook and is noted as conducted by the minister Ryder rather than
         Floud]

Folio 24 recto

109.   1740 May 22* John LUTWITCH of St Catherins Dry Cooper Widdower
         and Mary WATTS of the Pa. of Queenhith widdow at Mr Balls J Floud
         [*As to the date, see the note to entry 106. The true date is probably 22 October
         1728]
110.   22. Henry BAKER of St Martins in the Fields Tobacconist and Wid
         & Jane SYMS of St Margarets Westminster at Mr Balls Spinster J Floud Min

Folio 24 verso

111.   22. William GAGE of the Parish of Little Gadsdin in the County of Hertfordsh. Wid
         & Souldier & Barbary ONEEL of the same Widdow Mar: R Bow JF M
         [For 'R Bow' see my note to entry 9 above]
112.   23. Joseph SIMPSON of Clerkenwell Batchelor & Glover
         & Jane DOCK of Barnet sp Hartfordshire Mar Mrs Wilsons J Floyd Min

Folio 25 recto

113.   23. Nathaniel SYMS of the Parish of Walthamstow husbandman and Batchelor
         and Thomazin PAR Widdow of Rotherhith Married at the Gun in St Georges Field JF
         Min
114.   24. Thomas ALLEN of the Parish of Aldgate Butcher & Batchelor
         and Sarah TIPPETT of the same place Spinster Mar R Bow JF M
         [For 'R Bow' see my note to entry 9 above]

Folio 25 verso

115.   1728. 24. Mark FOX of the Parish of Shadwel St Pauls of the first Regiment of
       Guards and Hannah HEWS of the Pa. afforesaid Spinster Mar R Bow JF
       [For 'R Bow' see my note to entry 9 above]
116.   25. Philip LANE of the Parish of Banger in Hartfordsh. Miller and Batchelor
       & Mary GEVES of the Pa. of Watton* in the county afforesaid spinster J Floud
       *[*Possibly Walton]*

Folio 26 recto

117.   25. Henry VAUDERY Wolcomer of the Parish of Ashon* & Mercy Bank* in Cheshire
       & Anne GRIFFIN of the Pa. of Tosister in Northamptonshire Sp JF M at Mr Balls
       *[*The parishes of the spouses are probably Ashton upon Mersey and Towcester
       respectively]*
118.   25. Thomas BENNETT of the Pa. of Boxley near Maidstone in Kent Gardner and Ba
       and Martha COLEMAN of the same place spinster married JF Min

Folio 26 verso

119.   26. George BEAN wid of Shadwell seafaringman
       & Hannah PAINTER of Shadwell spinster at Mr Balls JF
120.   26. James HAMBRIDGE of the Pa. of Kensington Ba and Husbandman & Batchelor
       and Eliz: BURGES of Paddington Widdow were married at Mrs Wilsons By Lycence
       JF
       *[A rare reference to a marriage licence. A marriage licence issued by a church
       official would not have authorised a marriage in the environs of the Fleet, but Mr
       Floud and the couple may have ignored that part of the licence that specified the
       church (or churches) in which the marriage could take place. It is also possible
       that the licence was silent as to the place in which the couple should marry.
       Some Fleet parsons also issued their own licences (for a fee),although such a
       licence was invalid in the eyes of the church]*

Folio 27 recto

121.   26. Richard BRIDGES of the Pa. of Chatham*
       & Mary TOPLIFT of the Pa. of Plymouth in ye Devon Wid at P.
       RB Belongs to the Grafton man of war Ric HADDOCK Commander Mar: Mr Philips
       *[*In Kent. RB is presumably the groom, Richard BRIDGES. This entry is a good
       example of the detail often found in notebook entries. The minister has not only
       noted the name of the ship on which the groom was serving, but also the name of
       its commander]*
122.   26. Thomas BRISCOE of the Parish of dorkin* in the County of Kent husbandman
       & Batchelor and Catherine KING of the Parish of Great Buckhouse* in the County
       afforesaid Spinster JF Min. At the Ship on Fleet Ditch Lond. Cer: Dat 25 of April
       1728
       *[*The parishes of the spouses are probably Dorking and Great Bookham, which
       were both in Surrey. This entry is another example of Floud providing a backdated
       marriage certificate]*

Folio 27 verso

123.   28. James DAWLEN of the Parish of St Andrews Holborn Gent mans Ser: and Ba
       and Anne STREDWICK of the Parish of St Georges Hanover Square JF Min

124.   29. Andrew NICHOLS of the Parish of Stepney Marriner and Ba
        and Anne GRAHAM of the same place widdow
        Marr at Mrs Wilsons Cer: in the Pa. of St Sepulchers Lond
        *[This entry may mean that the couple were supplied with a marriage certificate
        that would imply to third parties that they were married at St Sepulchres, rather
        than by a Fleet parson at Mrs Wilsons' marriage shop in the Fleet]*

Folio 28 recto
125.   29. John CHAPPEL of the Pa. of Stepney Marriner & Batchelor
        and Mary CLEMENTS of the same place Spinster married at the 3 Crowns Ld
        Mayors Day JF Min. King street King Henry yard near Farthing fields near the Bird
        in Hand ale house
126.   29. Benjamin SHELTON of St Georges Hanover Square
        and Eliz RUDSON of the same place married By JF
127.   29. Jonathan TURF of St Georg's Wid & Anne HARWOOD of the Par of Lambeth
        widdow at Balls Mr Holdrites Brewer Jno Floyd Min

Folio 28 verso
128.   1728. 29. Richard PRICKTOE of St Martins in the Fields
        and Susannah GUILDER of the same place spinster JF Min
129.   29. Georg LEWSON Francis STONE and Anthony ELLIS
        & Su: STANLEY all of Stepney at the Vine JF Min
        *[This extraordinary entry may record two marriages conducted by Floud at the
        Vine; firstly the marriage of Georg LEWSON and Francis (or Frances) STONE and,
        secondly, the marriage of Anthony ELLIS and Susan (or Susannah) STANLEY]*
130.   29. Wm ROBERTS St Giles's Carpenter and Mary PRICE of the Pa.
        of St Sepulchers London at Mr Balls JF Min

Folio 29 recto
131.   30. John WOODCOCK of the Pa. of Alhallows Berkin by the Tower London Ba and
        Gent mans Servt. & Ales MITTCHEL of the Pa. of St Martins in the Field Sp: Mar at
        Mr Cliftons JF Min
132.   30. John TURNER of the Pa. of St Anns Westminster Ba: and Plaisterer
        and Mary WATKINS of the Pa. of St Bridgets London
        Mar at their own room at St Giles's JF Min
        *[This is one of the few entries that record the couple being married at their own
        home]*

Folio 29 verso
133.   1 November 1728. Henry CANHAM of ye Pa. of St Matthews Ipswitch Suffolk, wid
        & house carpenter and Francis SKINNER of Hartfield in Essex Sp: mar JF Min
134.   1. Henry COMFORT of the Pa. of St Martins in ye Fields Labourer and Ba
        & Eliz: DEAKINS of the Pa. of St Clements Dean Spinster Mar at Mr Balls JF M

Folio 30 recto
135.   2. Joseph HILL of St James's Labour and Ba & Mary REN of Kingston upon
        Thames* Sp at Wheelers JF Min
        *[*In Surrey]*

136.   3. Edward WILLIAMS of the Pa. of St Georges Southwark
        & Mary LETTENBIRG* of St Georges Southwark Labourer and Spinster JF Min
        [*The last few letters of the surname are unclear]
137.   3. John PILGRAM Carpenter of Kingsington parish widower
        & Elizabeth LEA of ye same widow JF Min

Folio 30 verso
138.   3. John RICHARDSON
        and Hannah FENNILOW at Mrs Wilsons and tie* Wilson there JF M
        [*This word is unclear]
139.   4. Thomas BANCE wid: of the Parish of Haster in the Hundred of Stow
        and Mary HOWARD of the same place wid J Floud Min

Folio 31 recto
140.   4. Joseph KEMP of St Clements Dean Plummer
        and Eliz: BUCKLEY of St Clements Dean Mar at Mrs Wilsons London JF M
141.   5. Joseph TREACHER of Busshea* Husbandman
        and Eliz: WILLIAMS of the same place Spinster Mar: at Mr Cliftons on the Ditch
        side JF M
        [*Probably Bushey in Hertfordshire]

Folio 31 verso
142.   5. William STROWD of the Pa. of Stepney framework knitter and Ba
        and Eliz BROWN of the same Sp Mar at Mr Clifton
143.   5. John LOW of the Pa. of St Martins in the Fields Cordwainer & Ba
        & Jane ANDDERSON of the same place Sp at Mr Gilberts JF M

Folio 32 recto
144.   5. Edward POTTLE of St Georg's Southwark Pipemaker and Ba
        & Anne PEACE of the same place Spinster Mar: at Mr Balls
        Edward RENNOLDS* Father near the Sun in the Burrow JF Min
        [*The entry does not make it clear who Edward RENNOLDS was, or why he is
        noted. He may have been the father of the bride, but he has a different surname
        from the bride who is noted as a spinster]
145.   5. Andrew DUNCANE 3 R G* of Col Sinclears company
        and Eliz KNIBLET of the Pa. of Covent Garden Mar at Mr Balls J Floyd Min
        [*Probably the 3 Regiment of Foot Guards]

Folio 32 verso
146.   5. Joseph CARPENTER of St Michaels Coventry* Cordwainer and Ba
        & Mabel HAMMONDS of the Pa. of St Andrews Holborn Sp
        married at Mr Cliftons JF
        [*In Warwickshire]
147.   6. George SHAW of the Pa. of St Mary Overy Brewers Servt and Ba
        and Eliz: BILLINGS Widdow of the same place at the Anchor and Crown JF Min

Folio 33 recto
148.   6. Jane SHEPPARD* of ye Pa. of St James's sp
and Roger GODDIN of Stepney Marriner JF M
[*This is one of the very few entries which have the name of the bride appearing first]

149.   6. John THOMAS of the Pa. of Milton near Siddenburn in Kent Batchelor and
Fisherman and Mary SMITH of the Parish of Earley in Berkshire Spinster
Mar: at Wilsons at ye Gallon pot Jno Floyd Min

Folio 33 verso
150.   7. Thomas ASMAL of the Pa. of Hornsey Sadler & Widdower
& Margaret COX of the Pa. of Greenwitch Widdow Married at the Fighting Cocks
Fleet Lane

151.   8. George SLEIGH* of Wappin Stepney Marriner and Ba
and Eliz BERLOW of the same Sp at Mr Balls JF M
[*This surname is smudged and could be SLOUGH]

Folio 34 recto
152.   8. Samuel WEST of the Parish of Stepney Batchelor & Marriner
and Eliz: AVILLION of the Pa. of Wappin Stepney Sp:
Mr Samuel COLLIERS* a Barber in Fleet Lane
[*Possibly a witness to the wedding, or the owner of the premises at which the ceremony took place]

153.   9. John COOK of the 2 Re of Guards
and Jane RICH of the Pa. of St Margaretts Westminster Wid at Mr Leveretts Fleet
Lane JF Min

Folio 34 verso
154.   9. William FRANCIS of the Parish of Wansworth* Husbandman & widdow
and Elizabeth TAPLIS of the same place Widdow Mar at the Winmill Jno Floyd Min
[*Probably Wandsworth in Surrey]

155.   10. Samuel WANT of the Parish of St Georges Hannover Square Coachman and
Batchelor and Francis BERRY of Crutched Fryers Sp Mar: at Mrs Wilsons
I promise to give a Parchment certificate without fee.
[A rare example of a certificate being given, or promised, without a further fee]

Folio 35 recto
156.   11. Henry BATTEN of the Pa. of Stepney Marriner & Batchelor
and Mary WOODHAM of the same Sp Mar at Mrs Wilsons JF Min
[See entry 651 in the register in RG 7/3]

157.   11. Richard STENNETT of the Pa. of Wotton near Darkin* Wid: & Husbandman
and Eliz: LIPSCOMBE of the same Mar at Mrs Wilsons JF Min
[*Dorking in Surrey. See also entry 652 in the register in RG 7/3]

Folio 35 verso
158.   1728. 11. Joseph LEAK of the Parish of White chappel Clockmaker and
Batchelor* Wid and Joanna HOWIT of the same place widdow Mar at Mrs Wilsons
JF Min
[*The word batchelor has been crossed out and wid has been written above it. See also entry 653 in the register in RG 7/3]

Folio 36 recto

159.   11. Thomas BELSHAM of the Pa. of Sevenoak in Kent Ba and Carpenter
and Eliz: HODGES of the same place or seal at the Blackhors Sp
married at the Green Lettice in the Burrow the Certificate Dat 11 Ap Last past JF M

Folio 36 verso

160.   12. Thomas BEACH of St Margaretts Westminster Batchelor & Buttcher
& Eliz: JOHNSON of the same place Sp at the Shepherd and Goat JF M

Folio 37 recto

161.   13. William WEVER of Stepney widdower and Mary BETHEL of Clerkinwell Sp at
Mr Balls JF Min Browns Lane Spittlefields near the Old Swan Alehouse Swan Alley

162.   13. Thomas LAWRENCE of St Clements Dean Blacksmith and widdowr
& Anne CATON of the same place Mar. at Mr Balls JF Min

Folio 37 verso

163.   13. John HOWSE of Clerkinwell
and Sarah PRESSLAND of the same Sp Mar at Mr Ball JF Min

164.   13. Samuel CHALLENGE of the Parish of St Sepulchers London Glassgrinder and
Ba & Jane LEA of the Parish afforesaid sp mar at the cock in the Oldbayley JF Min

Folio 38 recto

165.   14. George WEAR of the Parish of St James's Westminster Clothworker & Ba
and Mary TURNER of the same place wid Mar at Mrs Wilsons JF Min

166.   14. William BABBS of ye Pa. of Cripple Gate Ba & Farrier
& Anne BESLEY of the same Place Sp Mar at Mr Balls JF Min

Folio 38 verso

167.   1728. 14. John ORTON of the 3 Regiment of Gua.
and Martha NICHOLS of the Pa. of St Bridgets London
Mar at Mr Duncoms 10 a clock at night JF M
*[A rare example of an entry noting the time of the marriage. In this case, the
marriage was certainly outside of the canonical hours]*

168.   15. George RAMSEY of the Pa. of Shadwel marriner & Ba
and Margaret COLESTONE of the same place Widdow were mar at the Ship on ye
Ditch side Jno Floud Min

Folio 39 recto

169.   15. John PEARCE of the Pa. of St James Westminster Gent & Ba
& Eliz: FURNIS of the Pa. of St Martins in the Fields Spinster at ye R Bow JF Min
[For 'R Bow' see my note to entry 9 above]

Folio 39 verso

170.   Mr BULL* of East Bar???w in Hartfordsh.
*[*The surname is smudged and difficult to read. This entry is incomplete, or it
may be merely a note by Floud of someone's name and place of residence rather
than a marriage entry]*

171.   15. John WOODCOCK of St Georges Haberdasher of smallwares and wid
and Sarah CAMPION of the same place Sp.
Mar at George yard at their own rooms JF Min Dat 15 Novr. 1721
*[This is one of the few entries that record the couple being married at their own
home. It also appears that Floud gave the couple a certificate backdated by seven
years. The couple probably had a number of children and they wished to make all
of them appear to have been born in wedlock]*

Folio 40 recto
172.   16. Tho RYLAN wid Anne THOMAS Sp
173.   17. John PLOWMAN Eliz: BARNS Islinton Both Gents Serv. Batchelor & Sp
Whelers JF

Folio 40 verso
174.   17. Joseph SHEEPHERD* of Cripplegt
and Catherine HARRIOTT of St Ollive Silver Street Ba & Sp Married at Wilsons JF
Min
*[*Possibly a mistake for SHEPHERD]*
175.   17. Matthew SAVAGE of the Pa. of St Gileses Cooper
and Ales BLAND of the same Ba & Sp Anchor & Crown JF

Folio 41 recto
176.   17. John MARSH of Cripplegate Labourer and Mary HARLEY wid wid
at the Anchor and Crown JF Min
177.   17. James JOHNSTONE of the Precinct of Bridewell Ba and Perukemaker
and Mary COWARD of the same place Spinster
Mar at ye White Horse Inn near Holborn Bridge Lond J Floud Min

Folio 41 verso
178.   17. Timothy NEWBERRY of the Parish of St Ollive near London in ye County of
Surrey Merchant & Ba and Lydia BAGLY of the Pa. afforesaid sp
Married at Mr Corbetts JF Min
[See also entry 725 in the register in RG 7/3]
179.   18. John MILTON of the Pa. of Hickenham in the County of Mdx Ba and
Husbandman & Blacksmith & Sarah CRAYFORD of the same place sp Married at
the signe of the golden Ball in seacoal Lane London Richard FRICHLEY* man of the
house JF Min
*[*This surname is smudged and very difficult to read. He is probably the
proprietor of the tavern]*

Folio 42 recto
180.   18. John EDWARDS of the Pa. of St Giles's* Cripple Gate Marriner and Joyner and
Batchelor and Sarah RENNOLDS of the same place spinster Married at Mrs
Wilsons JF Min
*[*The words 'in the Fields' have been written, then crossed out, and 'Cripple Gate'
written at the time of the rest of the entry. See also entry 723 in the register in RG
7/3]*

Folio 42 verso
181.   19. John WESTWOOD of Acton Husbandman & Ba
       & Mary WRIGHT of the same place widdow Married at Mr Balls J Floud Min
182.   19. John LEONARD of the Pa. of St Ollive By the Bridge Seafaring man and Ba
       and Anne CROUCH of St Ollive afforesaid Sp
       Married at the Boreshead in Stonecutters Street JF Min

Folio 43 recto
183.   20. William GRACE of the Parish of Bishops Gate Barber Surgeon & wid
       and Mary OBBS* of the Pa. of St Giles's in the Fields the Criple Widdow
       Mar at Mr Balls JF Min
       *[*Probably a mistake for HOBBS. The words 'in the Fields' have been crossed out
       and 'the Criple' written, in the same hand, in the margin]*
184.   20. Walter TAYLOR of the Pa. of St Giles ye Cripple Glover & Ba
       and Sarah CARLILE of the Pa. afforesaid Sp
       Mar ye 20 and the certificate Dat 20 Nover 1723 at Balls JF Min
       *[Floud provided this couple with a certificate backdated by five years. See also
       entry 171]*

Folio 43 verso
185.   20. Benjamin MORGAN of the Pa. of Aldgate Batchelor & Seafaringman
       and Jane GREEN of the same place sp Mar at Mr Cliftons at Cliftons JF Min
186.   21. John MARTIN of the Pa. of Shoreditch
       and Eliz: GODDARD of the same place Sp at the Barly mow married JF
       [See also entry 657 in the register in RG 7/3]

Folio 44 recto
187.   21. James LEA of the Pa. of St Giles's in the Fields Ba and Weaver
       and Martha ELSON of the same place widdow were married no certificate Mrs
       Wilsons JF Min
188.   Dec 1 1728*. Nicholas GARRETT of St Sepulchers porter & wid
       and Anne WALKER of the Pa. of Bishops Gate widow wid Mrs Wilsons
       *[*This entry for December 1728 appears to have been inserted later, but in the
       same hand as most of the entries in this notebook. The next entry is dated '21'
       and so appears to carry on the sequence from entry 187]*
189.   21*. Henry COPNER of St James's Westminster and Elliner FROST sp Mar 26 Feb
       1727 on the first leaf of the Register
       *[*Probably 21 November (see note to entry 188), but the text of the entry
       suggests that this marriage took place in February 1727]*
190.   Lacy NETTLESHIP Pancrass Eliz TWITCHEN of the same
       *[It is unclear if this is an entry for a marriage, but it is in the same handwriting as
       most of the entries in the notebook]*

Folio 44 verso
191.   1728. 22. John EVANS and Eliza: JOHNSON of Cheanis in Buckingham shire and
       John of the same Ba & Sp Mar at Mr Balls JF
192.   22. John CHRISTIAN of the Pa. of St Giles's Cripplegate Packthred Spinner and Ba
       and Sharlot SHEPHERD of the Pa. aforesaid Sp Mar: Barly Mow JF Min

Folio 45 recto

193.   1728. Richard MAY & Anne SOUTHHALL married in an all* in Shoe Lane 1728
*[*Possibly a reference to a hall. This entry is in a different hand to most of the entries in this notebook]*

194.   30 of Novr 1728. Edward CHAPMAN of Lucam Kent
and Sarah WADLEY of the Pa. of St Andrews Holborn
Mar at the Goat and Crown near St Georges Church

195.   A Cupple Married at Mr Fillips's on the 22nd of August 1726 ye Certificate Dated on the same day of the month Dated 1722
Richard DIMMERY of the pa of St Tho. Bristol* and Jane REASON of St Mary Nottingham Spinster at Phillips'
*[*In Gloucestershire. This entry is upside down on the lower half of the page. The date of the entry is two years earlier than other entries in the notebook and the minister notes that he provided the couple with a certificate backdated by four years]*

Folio 45 verso

196.   30*. 1728. Henry MARES soldier and Eliz: JONES Sp at Mr Cliftons JF
*[*Probably November]*

197.   1 Dec: 1728. Wm STATCHBERRY of the Pa. of New Branford Husband man and Ba and Mary VINCENT of the Pa. of Twitnam Spinster JF Min

198.   Dec 8th 1728 Johnnathan HOPWOOD of the Pa. of Luisham*
and Mary SPENCER of the same Wid and Wid: Mar at ye winmill JF Min
*[*Probably Lewisham in Kent. This is the last entry in the notebook in the handwriting of most of the entries above. All the entries that follow (and entries 1, 2, 3, and 193 above) are in a common hand and may have been added after John Floud had finished with the notebook (he died about a year after this entry). See also entry 670 in the register in RG 7/3]*

Folio 46 recto

199.   Decemb. 1* 1728 Will SMITH son of John and Ann SMITH was baptized at ye Red Cross in Newgate Street near court** JT
*[*Possibly 7. **This word is difficult to read. JT is probably John Tarrant. See my note to entry 198 above in respect of the handwriting of this entry. This baptism appears at entry 585 in the register in RG 7/3. This last (paper) page of the notebook, seems to have originally been headed 'October', but was later written over with 'Decemb'. It may be that the date of this baptism was originally recorded as October 1728, but the clerk or minister who filled in the last few pages of this notebook with marriages needed the page for December marriages and so he simply changed the heading of the page at 46 recto. If this is correct, it may explain why the baptism was inserted by a clerk into the register in RG 7/3 under the month of October (at entry 585), in between the entries of marriage from this notebook which appear as 72 and 73 above]*

200.   Dec 8 Tho BEACH of the 2 Regmet of Guards
& Mary HOLLAND of ye Parish of Chelsea Sp mari Sunday at Balls JF
[See my note to entry 198 above in respect of the handwriting of this entry]

201.   John BLAKE Brickmaker of St George hannover Sq Bat
and Mary CRUTHLEY of ye same Sp one new years day 1726
[See my note to entry 198 above in respect of the handwriting of this entry]

Folio 46 verso

202.   18. 1728. Thomas LEWIS of ye Parish of St Sepulchers Cord & Bat
and Susannah SHEPARD of Do Sp Jno Floud min at mrs Willson
[See my note to entry 198 above in respect of the handwriting of this entry]

203.   John EVINS & Eliz COATS Carteret Garys
[See my note to entry 198 above in respect of the handwriting of this entry]

204.   Samuel ELWOOD of ye 1st Regment of Gurdes Bat
& Eliz WILLMOTH of St Olives Spinster were married in ye mint JT*
[*Probably the minister John Tarrant. This marriage is recorded as having taken place at the Mint, an area in Southwark near the King's Bench Prison – see the introduction to this volume. See my note to entry 198 above in respect of the handwriting of this entry. See also entry 619 in the register in RG 7/3]

Folio 47 recto (inside back cover)

205.   1728. Dec 24. George GRESSHAM & Mary JONES ???* JONES ???* at Balls
[*These words are illegible. See my note to entry 198 above in respect of the handwriting of this entry]

206.   Will STEPHENS Waterman and Mary BLAKE New* Ch??* ????* 3 years agoe
[*These words are illegible. See my note to entry 198 above in respect of the handwriting of this entry]

End of notebook in piece RG 7/563

Index to places

This index refers the reader to the numbers of those entries in the registers and notebook (or my notes to each entry) that specify an English county (other than Middlesex) or Welsh county as a spouse's place of residence. The entries in these registers and notebook do not refer to any places outside England and Wales. In some cases, the ministers or clerks who prepared the registers and notebook did not record the name of a spouse's county of residence because it was the same, or very similar, to the name of that spouse's town or city; e.g. Bedford, Cambridge, Lancaster, Oxford and York. In those cases, I have included the entries in the index under the county name.

526, 537, 547, 555,
572, 576, 578, 650,
652, 691, 706, 708,
709, 725.
RG 7/163: 1, 14.
RG 7/563: 5, 6, 12, 23,
25, 33, 41, 58, 62, 65,
122, 135, 154, 157,
178.
Sussex
RG 7/3: 21, 412, 479.
RG 7/163: 40.
Warwickshire
RG 7/3: 521.
RG 7/563: 7, 146.
Wiltshire
RG 7/3: 47, 424, 584.
RG 7/563: 50, 72.
Yorkshire
RG 7/3: 696.

Welsh counties
Denbigh
RG 7/3: 142, 722.
Montgomery
RG 7/3: 508.
Pembroke
RG 7/3: 508.

Index to surnames

This index refers the reader to the numbers of those entries in the registers and notebook (or my notes to each entry) that include the surnames listed below. I have not included the names of the officiating ministers or the names of the owners of the marriage houses at which the ceremonies were preformed.

Becket; RG 7/3: 146
Beddall; RG 7/3: 696
Bedford; RG 7/3: 676
Beldum; RG 7/3: 36 RG
  7/163: 118
Bell; RG 7/3: 440, 583 RG
  7/563: 71
Belsham; RG 7/563: 159
Benfield; RG 7/3: 486
Bennet; RG 7/3: 284 RG
  7/563: 68
Bennett; RG 7/3: 157,
  294, 310, 559, 580 RG
  7/563: 45, 118
Bentley; RG 7/563: 87
Bently; RG 7/3: 600
Berlow; RG 7/563: 151
Berry; RG 7/3: 250, 416
  RG 7/563: 155
Besford; RG 7/163: 49
Besley; RG 7/563: 166
Best; RG 7/163: 4
Bethel; RG 7/563: 161
Betts; RG 7/3: 691
Bibby; RG 7/3: 383
Biddell; RG 7/3: 381
Biggs; RG 7/3: 456, 516
Bignold; RG 7/163: 102
Bigs; RG 7/3: 630 RG
  7/563: 3
Bill; RG 7/3: 184, 649
Billing; RG 7/3: 37
Billings; RG 7/563: 147
Billingsly; RG 7/163: 106
Bird; RG 7/3: 581 RG
  7/563: 69
Bisbrown; RG 7/3: 483
Blackborn; RG 7/3: 518 RG
  7/563: 4
Blackmore; RG 7/3: 251
Blake; RG 7/3: 98, 134 RG
  7/563: 201, 206
Bland; RG 7/563: 175
Blewitt; RG 7/3: 659
Blondal; RG 7/3: 492
Bloss; RG 7/3: 187
Blunden; RG 7/3: 259
Bodall; RG 7/3: 363
Bolton; RG 7/3: 132, 416
Boman; RG 7/3: 664
Bonibridge; RG 7/3: 245
Bonney; RG 7/3: 445

Boock; RG 7/3: 437
Boot; RG 7/3: 386
Boswell; RG 7/3: 123
Botthamly; RG 7/3: 292
Bourn; RG 7/3: 636
Bowator; RG 7/3: 463
Bowden; RG 7/3: 404
Bowen; RG 7/3: 392
Bowie; RG 7/163: 100
Bowler; RG 7/3: 182
Bowles; RG 7/3: 183
Bows; RG 7/3: 146
Bowser; RG 7/3: 413
Bowyer; RG 7/3: 10, 19,
  21
Boyen; RG 7/3: 449
Boze; RG 7/3: 542 RG
  7/563: 28
Bradberry; RG 7/563: 18
Bradbury; RG 7/3: 532
Bradfield; RG 7/3: 641
Bradley; RG 7/3: 177
Brain; RG 7/3: 203
Brand; RG 7/3: 312
Brasier; RG 7/3: 315
Breleibon; RG 7/3: 350
Brewer; RG 7/3: 702
Bridges; RG 7/563: 121
Briggs; RG 7/3: 305
Brightwell; RG 7/3: 583
Brinkinfe; RG 7/3: 286
Briscoe; RG 7/563: 122
Bristow; RG 7/163: 51
Britewell; RG 7/563: 71
Brodix; RG 7/3: 340
Brooke; RG 7/3: 557
Brooks; RG 7/3: 181, 355,
  557 RG 7/563: 43
Broom; RG 7/3: 139
Broome; RG 7/3: 271
Brown; RG 7/3: 62, 116,
  151, 152, 172, 234,
  366 RG 7/163: 105 RG
  7/563: 142
Browning; RG 7/3: 340
Bruce; RG 7/3: 634
Brudenell; RG 7/3: 678,
  720
Brush; RG 7/3: 246
Bryan; RG 7/3: 26
Bscott; RG 7/3: 527
Buckingham; RG 7/3: 489

Buckland; RG 7/3: 93
Buckley; RG 7/563: 140
Buckman; RG 7/3: 490
Bullman; RG 7/3: 594
Bullmore; RG 7/3: 504
Bulman; RG 7/563: 81
Buly; RG 7/3: 616, 717 RG
  7/563: 104
Burges; RG 7/563: 120
Burgoine; RG 7/163: 48
Burlin; RG 7/3: 565 RG
  7/563: 51
Burn; RG 7/563: 85
Burne; RG 7/3: 598
Burridge; RG 7/3: 388
Burton; RG 7/3: 185, 204,
  634
Butler; RG 7/3: 709
Butsel; RG 7/3: 497
Butterfield; RG 7/3: 56
Byford; RG 7/3: 552 RG
  7/563: 38
Cambell; RG 7/3: 458
Campbell; RG 7/3: 524,
  704 RG 7/563: 10
Campion; RG 7/563: 171
Canham; RG 7/563: 133
Cann; RG 7/163: 65
Canning; RG 7/3: 584 RG
  7/563: 72
Cansley; RG 7/3: 231, 344
Cant; RG 7/3: 66
Cantrill; RG 7/3: 528 RG
  7/563: 14
Care; RG 7/3: 414
Carey; RG 7/3: 534 RG
  7/163: 43 RG 7/563: 20,
  21
Carlile; RG 7/563: 184
Carney; RG 7/3: 334
Carpenter; RG 7/563: 146
Carraffe; RG 7/163: 52
Carraway; RG 7/3: 288
Carrey; RG 7/3: 534
Carseley; RG 7/163: 2
Carter; RG 7/3: 115, 229,
  291
Caruthis; RG 7/3: 385
Carvel; RG 7/3: 496
Casalar; RG 7/163: 8
Casey; RG 7/3: 54
Cass; RG 7/3: 428

Casteen; RG 7/3: 240
Caten; RG 7/3: 393
Caton; RG 7/563: 162
Caward; RG 7/3: 724
Cawood; RG 7/3: 586 RG 7/563: 73
Cecil; RG 7/3: 296
Chalkley; RG 7/3: 297
Challenge; RG 7/563: 164
Chambers; RG 7/563: 101
Chapman; RG 7/563: 194
Chappel; RG 7/563: 125
Chappell; RG 7/3: 683
Charelleirett; RG 7/3: 241
Charreton; RG 7/3: 718
Chathley; RG 7/3: 297
Chester; RG 7/3: 303
Child; RG 7/3: 277
Chipperton; RG 7/3: 218
Christian; RG 7/563: 192
Chriswell; RG 7/563: 104
Church; RG 7/3: 86
Cirby; RG 7/3: 472
Cirwood; RG 7/3: 480
Cisil; RG 7/3: 296
Clack; RG 7/3: 102
Clare; RG 7/3: 195
Clark; RG 7/3: 138, 252, 435, 624 RG 7/163: 71
Clarke; RG 7/3: 51, 386, 406
Clayton; RG 7/3: 156, 466 RG 7/163: 40, 75
Cleaver; RG 7/3: 329
Clements; RG 7/163: 33 RG 7/563: 125
Clifford; RG 7/3: 517 RG 7/563: 3
Clifton; RG 7/3: 210
Clive; RG 7/3: 686
Cloebatch; RG 7/3: 8
Coats; RG 7/3: 264 RG 7/563: 203
Cobby; RG 7/3: 412
Cockram; RG 7/3: 394
Cocks; RG 7/3: 402 RG 7/163: 82
Cokayne; RG 7/163: 111
Cole; RG 7/3: 25, 49, 279
Coleman; RG 7/563: 118
Colestone; RG 7/563: 168
Coley; RG 7/3: 281, 614

RG 7/563: 100
Colgrove; RG 7/3: 383
Collier; RG 7/163: 50
Colliers; RG 7/563: 152
Collin; RG 7/3: 558 RG 7/563: 44
Collings; RG 7/3: 15, 498, 644
Collins; RG 7/3: 143
Collison; RG 7/163: 112
Combridg; RG 7/3: 711
Comfort; RG 7/563: 134
Comingham; RG 7/3: 273
Comson; RG 7/563: 108
Conner; RG 7/3: 549 RG 7/563: 35
Connyer; RG 7/3: 701
Cook; RG 7/3: 230, 347, 438, 468 RG 7/563: 153
Cooke; RG 7/3: 126, 476
Cooper; RG 7/3: 283, 503
Copethore; RG 7/163: 90
Copner; RG 7/563: 189
Corbett; RG 7/3: 30, 43
Cork; RG 7/163: 42
Corner; RG 7/3: 668
Corningham; RG 7/3: 273
Costick; RG 7/163: 54
Cottell; RG 7/3: 93
Cottrell; RG 7/3: 169
Courtee; RG 7/3: 216
Coventery; RG 7/3: 688
Coward; RG 7/563: 177
Cowdwell; RG 7/3: 712
Cox; RG 7/3: 596 RG 7/563: 83, 150
Crackwell; RG 7/3: 339
Crafford; RG 7/163: 111
Crawley; RG 7/3: 103, 164
Cray; RG 7/3: 178, 349
Crayford; RG 7/563: 179
Creed; RG 7/3: 589 RG 7/563: 76
Criswell; RG 7/3: 616, 717
Crone; RG 7/3: 455
Crosbey; RG 7/3: 46
Crosby; RG 7/3: 41
Crossley; RG 7/3: 139
Crouch; RG 7/3: 42 RG 7/563: 182
Crowder; RG 7/3: 710
Crowdirs; RG 7/3: 600 RG

7/563: 87
Crowley; RG 7/3: 82
Crowser; RG 7/3: 716
Crumer; RG 7/3: 300
Cruthley; RG 7/563: 201
Cubbidge; RG 7/3: 220
Cunningham; RG 7/163: 27
Curtis; RG 7/3: 45, 541 RG 7/563: 27
Cuthbert; RG 7/3: 434
Dackombe; RG 7/163: 68
Dale; RG 7/3: 323, 402
Dalton; RG 7/3: 10, 54
Daniel; RG 7/3: 365
Danison; RG 7/3: 233
Darbey; RG 7/3: 580
Darby; RG 7/563: 68
Darling; RG 7/3: 311
Dashwood; RG 7/3: 166
Davidson; RG 7/3: 471
Davis; RG 7/3: 188, 253, 258, 299, 307, 313, 395, 533, 601, 615, 704, 722 RG 7/163: 53, 117, 118 RG 7/563: 19, 88, 102
Dawlen; RG 7/563: 123
Dawson; RG 7/3: 31, 325, 506
Day; RG 7/3: 103, 505
Deacon; RG 7/3: 501
Deakers; RG 7/3: 570 RG 7/563: 56
Deakins; RG 7/563: 134
Dean; RG 7/3: 85
Deanne; RG 7/3: 102
Deargg; RG 7/163: 115
De Hone; RG 7/3: 320
Delany; RG 7/3: 367
Deman; RG 7/3: 610 RG 7/563: 96
Denegall; RG 7/163: 96
Denis; RG 7/163: 113
Denning; RG 7/163: 113
Dennis; RG 7/3: 254
Dent; RG 7/3: 550 RG 7/563: 36
Derrick; RG 7/3: 370
Dickerson; RG 7/3: 282
Dickson; RG 7/3: 135
Dillen; RG 7/3: 349

Dillew; RG 7/3: 179
Dimmery; RG 7/563: 195
Dixon; RG 7/3: 531 RG 7/563: 17
Dobson; RG 7/3: 59
Dock; RG 7/563: 112
Dod; RG 7/3: 215
Dollard; RG 7/163: 74
Dolley; RG 7/3: 255
Dorcap; RG 7/3: 590
Dorcass; RG 7/3: 590 RG 7/563: 77
Dorrington; RG 7/3: 122
Douglas; RG 7/163: 14
Dove; RG 7/3: 22
Dowglas; RG 7/3: 69
Downs; RG 7/3: 648
Doyle; RG 7/3: 190
Dublack; RG 7/163: 13
Dudley; RG 7/3: 114
Duglas; RG 7/163: 14
Duglass; RG 7/3: 490
Dunbar; RG 7/3: 275
Dunbarr; RG 7/3: 626
Duncane; RG 7/563: 145
Dunman; RG 7/3: 571
Dunmar; RG 7/3: 571 RG 7/563: 57
Dunstan; RG 7/3: 318
Durant; RG 7/3: 435
Durantt; RG 7/3: 125
Duson; RG 7/3: 77
Dwyer; RG 7/3: 378
Eades; RG 7/3: 420
Eadnell; RG 7/163: 38
Eady; RG 7/3: 217
Eams; RG 7/3: 302
Earle; RG 7/3: 594 RG 7/563: 81
East; RG 7/3: 68
Eaton; RG 7/3: 80, 625
Edgerton; RG 7/163: 26
Edmonds; RG 7/3: 636
Edward; RG 7/3: 367
Edwards; RG 7/3: 136, 277, 333, 432, 584, 723 RG 7/563: 72, 180
Eldridge; RG 7/3: 323, 357
Eling; RG 7/3: 53
Eliott; RG 7/3: 360, 433
Elkans; RG 7/163: 119
Elles; RG 7/3: 720

Ellis; RG 7/3: 232, 544, 678 RG 7/563: 1, 30, 129
Elmer; RG 7/3: 65
Elner; RG 7/3: 441
Elson; RG 7/563: 187
Elwood; RG 7/3: 619 RG 7/563: 204
Emerton; RG 7/3: 480
Emley; RG 7/3: 30
Emmerson; RG 7/3: 535 RG 7/563: 21
England; RG 7/3: 672, 696
Engrove; RG 7/3: 90
Enly; RG 7/3: 443
Ericke; RG 7/3: 439
Eston; RG 7/3: 376
Etheridge; RG 7/3: 155
Evanes; RG 7/3: 309
Evans; RG 7/3: 164, 464 RG 7/563: 191
Everet; RG 7/3: 499
Everton; RG 7/3: 644 RG 7/163: 32
Evins; RG 7/3: 185, 186, 240, 256 RG 7/563: 203
Falkner; RG 7/3: 148, 150
Fanning; RG 7/3: 190
Farmer; RG 7/3: 693
Farrmer; RG 7/3: 661
Fear; RG 7/3: 368
Feling; RG 7/3: 207
Felows; RG 7/3: 83, 488
Fenley; RG 7/3: 86
Fenner; RG 7/3: 157
Fennick; RG 7/3: 397
Fennilow; RG 7/563: 138
Fhreeves; RG 7/3: 623
Field; RG 7/3: 85, 268
Figan; RG 7/3: 491
Figgers; RG 7/3: 293
Fillabrown; RG 7/3: 444
Finmore; RG 7/163: 1
Firth; RG 7/3: 112, 599 RG 7/563: 86
Fish; RG 7/3: 213
Fisher; RG 7/3: 202, 719
Fleming; RG 7/3: 634
Fletcher; RG 7/3: 302 RG 7/163: 79
Flood; RG 7/3: 522
Floudgate; RG 7/3: 611 RG

7/563: 97
Flow; RG 7/3: 561
Folkner; RG 7/3: 353
Foot; RG 7/3: 60
Ford; RG 7/3: 471
Fort; RG 7/3: 488
Foster; RG 7/3: 67, 79, 89, 200, 227, 597 RG 7/563: 84
Fostin; RG 7/3: 88
Fox; RG 7/3: 16, 158, 698 RG 7/563: 115
Francis; RG 7/3: 578 RG 7/163: 108 RG 7/563: 65, 154
Francisco; RG 7/3: 286
Franklin; RG 7/3: 71, 158, 176, 546 RG 7/563: 32
Frasier; RG 7/3: 193
Frawhock; RG 7/3: 81
Freeman; RG 7/3: 67, 96, 155, 357, 566 RG 7/563: 52
Freerton; RG 7/3: 57
Freman; RG 7/3: 380
French; RG 7/3: 448
Freshwater; RG 7/3: 364
Frichley; RG 7/563: 179
Fricker; RG 7/3: 419
Friend; RG 7/163: 82
Frith; RG 7/3: 474
Frolick; RG 7/3: 99
Frost; RG 7/3: 68, 120 RG 7/563: 189
Fuller; RG 7/3: 107, 174, 502 RG 7/163: 61
Furnis; RG 7/563: 169
Furticue; RG 7/3: 697
Gage; RG 7/563: 111
Gale; RG 7/163: 19
Gallaghar; RG 7/3: 451
Gallington; RG 7/3: 380
Games; RG 7/3: 384
Gardener; RG 7/3: 172
Gardiner; RG 7/3: 152, 685 RG 7/163: 2
Gardner; RG 7/3: 38, 256, 505, 567, 606, 607 RG 7/563: 53, 93
Garland; RG 7/563: 107
Garrett; RG 7/563: 188
Gary; RG 7/3: 671

Gaskill; RG 7/3: 686
Gay; RG 7/3: 87
Gaynon; RG 7/163: 4
Geary; RG 7/163: 60
Geering; RG 7/163: 98
George; RG 7/163: 28
Gerinott; RG 7/3: 676
Geves; RG 7/563: 116
Ghislin; RG 7/163: 87
Gibbs; RG 7/3: 110
Gibbson; RG 7/3: 177
Gilbeartson; RG 7/563: 67
Gilbec; RG 7/163: 24
Gilbert; RG 7/3: 242
Gilbertson; RG 7/563: 103
Giles; RG 7/3: 76, 504
Gill; RG 7/3: 208, 451
Gillam; RG 7/3: 603 RG
   7/563: 90
Gille; RG 7/3: 460
Gillett; RG 7/3: 631
Ginn; RG 7/3: 332
Gipson; RG 7/3: 590 RG
   7/563: 77
Gislin; RG 7/163: 87
Gladwin; RG 7/3: 199
Glover; RG 7/3: 418
Gobart; RG 7/3: 586 RG
   7/563: 73
Goddard; RG 7/3: 553,
   657 RG 7/563: 39, 186
Goddin; RG 7/563: 148
Godfrey; RG 7/3: 482
Golby; RG 7/3: 131
Good; RG 7/3: 417
Goodacher; RG 7/3: 509
Goodale; RG 7/163: 98
Goodall; RG 7/3: 135, 361
Gooding; RG 7/3: 642
Goodman; RG 7/3: 263,
   675 RG 7/163: 39
Goolding; RG 7/163: 67
Goope; RG 7/3: 538
Gore; RG 7/3: 143, 309
Gormer; RG 7/3: 486
Gorring; RG 7/3: 274
Gosham; RG 7/3: 556 RG
   7/563: 42
Goslin; RG 7/3: 632
Gosnell; RG 7/3: 300
Goy; RG 7/3: 87
Grace; RG 7/3: 346 RG

7/563: 183
Graham; RG 7/563: 124
Grape; RG 7/3: 538 RG
   7/563: 24
Gratey; RG 7/3: 228, 346
Gravenor; RG 7/3: 404
Graves; RG 7/3: 137
Gravet; RG 7/3: 572 RG
   7/563: 58
Gray; RG 7/3: 322, 389,
   411, 573 RG 7/163: 7
   RG 7/563: 59
Greem; RG 7/3: 674
Green; RG 7/3: 6, 94, 119,
   153, 243, 244, 287,
   337, 345, 407, 646,
   656, 674 RG 7/563: 185
Greenaway; RG 7/3: 328
Greenleaf; RG 7/3: 296
Greenway; RG 7/3: 184
Gregory; RG 7/3: 205
Gressham; RG 7/563: 205
Greyston; RG 7/3: 76
Griffin; RG 7/3: 58, 495 RG
   7/163: 10 RG 7/563:
   117
Griffis; RG 7/3: 508
Griffith; RG 7/163: 100
Grimston; RG 7/163: 27
Groom; RG 7/3: 140
Groome; RG 7/3: 60
Gross; RG 7/3: 603 RG
   7/563: 90
Grubb; RG 7/163: 65
Grynes; RG 7/3: 301
Guest; RG 7/3: 97
Guffeck; RG 7/3: 261
Guilder; RG 7/563: 128
Guildfored; RG 7/3: 496
Guilford; RG 7/3: 201
Gunston; RG 7/3: 237
Guston; RG 7/3: 188
Haclin; RG 7/3: 537
Hadderwick; RG 7/3: 598
   RG 7/563: 85
Haddock; RG 7/563: 121
Haines; RG 7/3: 117
Halbrow; RG 7/3: 588 RG
   7/563: 75
Halden; RG 7/3: 324
Hale; RG 7/3: 29
Halfhead; RG 7/3: 467

Hall; RG 7/3: 18, 225,
   262, 274, 371, 393,
   575, 621, 658, 690 RG
   7/163: 3, 37, 105 RG
   7/563: 61
Hallin; RG 7/3: 537, 576,
   708 RG 7/563: 23, 62
Haloway; RG 7/3: 462
Hambridge; RG 7/563:
   120
Hamell; RG 7/3: 626
Hames; RG 7/163: 77
Hammond; RG 7/3: 579
   RG 7/563: 66
Hammonds; RG 7/563:
   146
Hamond; RG 7/3: 289
Hannan; RG 7/3: 370
Hanscomb; RG 7/3: 511
Harbutt; RG 7/3: 55
Harcott; RG 7/3: 95
Harderwick; RG 7/3: 598
Hardom; RG 7/3: 573 RG
   7/563: 59
Hardwitch; RG 7/3: 461
Hardy; RG 7/3: 401
Harley; RG 7/563: 176
Harper; RG 7/3: 19, 123,
   270, 534 RG 7/563: 20,
   21
Harrington; RG 7/3: 130
Harriott; RG 7/563: 174
Harris; RG 7/3: 192
Harrison; RG 7/3: 40, 49
Hart; RG 7/3: 31, 199 RG
   7/163: 60
Hartley; RG 7/3: 401
Harvey; RG 7/163: 64, 93
Harwood; RG 7/563: 127
Hatton; RG 7/3: 498
Hawkins; RG 7/3: 16
Haydon; RG 7/3: 552 RG
   7/563: 38
Hayes; RG 7/3: 317
Haylock; RG 7/3: 564 RG
   7/563: 50
Haynes; RG 7/3: 200
Hayward; RG 7/3: 501
Hazzard; RG 7/3: 35
Head; RG 7/3: 515, 628
   RG 7/563: 2
Heale; RG 7/563: 37

Healey; RG 7/3: 551
Heaththorne; RG 7/3: 206
Helbert; RG 7/163: 97
Hend; RG 7/3: 515
Henfield; RG 7/3: 522 RG
7/563: 8
Henkes; RG 7/3: 721
Henley; RG 7/3: 655
Herbert; RG 7/3: 413
Hewett; RG 7/3: 410
Hewit; RG 7/3: 165, 168
Hews; RG 7/3: 29, 52 RG
7/563: 115
Hicks; RG 7/163: 112,
114
Hide; RG 7/3: 299
Higgest; RG 7/3: 27
Higgs; RG 7/3: 20, 194
Hill; RG 7/3: 39, 147, 148,
209, 352, 353, 430,
649 RG 7/563: 135
Hines; RG 7/163: 26
Hinfield; RG 7/3: 707
Hinkley; RG 7/3: 578 RG
7/563: 65
Hinton; RG 7/3: 513
Hiram; RG 7/163: 13
Hirst; RG 7/3: 292
Hitchcock; RG 7/3: 163
Hive; RG 7/3: 574 RG
7/563: 60
Hoadley; RG 7/3: 37
Hobbs; RG 7/3: 215 RG
7/563: 183
Hobson; RG 7/3: 35
Hodges; RG 7/3: 23, 408
RG 7/563: 159
Hodgson; RG 7/163: 55
Hoggins; RG 7/3: 368
Holden; RG 7/3: 659
Holingsworth; RG 7/3: 445
Holland; RG 7/3: 13, 671
RG 7/563: 200
Holmes; RG 7/3: 613, 638
RG 7/563: 99
Holton; RG 7/3: 333
Honder; RG 7/3: 105
Hone; RG 7/3: 320
Hood; RG 7/3: 510, 522,
707 RG 7/563: 8
Hooper; RG 7/3: 77, 564
Hoopper; RG 7/563: 50

Hopkins; RG 7/3: 622
Hopwood; RG 7/3: 670 RG
7/563: 198
Hornwell; RG 7/3: 285
Horton; RG 7/3: 301
Hosgood; RG 7/3: 592 RG
7/563: 79
Hougdh; RG 7/3: 632
Hough; RG 7/3:632
Houlding; RG 7/3: 304
Houlterrice; RG 7/3: 426
Hovid; RG 7/3: 454
How; RG 7/3: 278, 561 RG
7/563: 47
Howard; RG 7/3: 117,
187, 306, 673 RG
7/563: 139
Howit; RG 7/3: 653 RG
7/563: 158
Howse; RG 7/563: 163
Hubbard; RG 7/3: 192
Hudson; RG 7/3: 396, 643
Huggins; RG 7/3: 231, 344
Hull; RG 7/3: 262, 305,
373
Humber; RG 7/3: 450
Humble; RG 7/3: 431
Hume; RG 7/3: 234
Hummerstone; RG 7/3:
186
Humphrey; RG 7/3: 695
Humphreys; RG 7/3: 78 RG
7/163: 93
Humphry; RG 7/3: 446
Hunt; RG 7/3: 389, 425
RG 7/163: 20
Hunter; RG 7/163: 63
Hurnall; RG 7/163: 116
Hurst; RG 7/163: 46
Hurste; RG 7/3: 426
Hurton; RG 7/3: 107
Hust; RG 7/163: 46
Hutchins; RG 7/3: 520,
575 RG 7/563: 6, 61
Hutchinson; RG 7/3: 221,
248
Hutton; RG 7/3: 518 RG
7/563: 4
Ice; RG 7/3: 439
Icomb; RG 7/3: 595
Iling; RG 7/3: 459
Imber; RG 7/3: 313

Inwood; RG 7/3: 640
Ireland; RG 7/3: 680
Irwin; RG 7/163: 38
Ivory; RG 7/163: 59
Jackeman; RG 7/3: 165
Jackson; RG 7/3: 9, 61,
115, 391, 500 RG
7/163: 31, 51
Jacobs; RG 7/163: 15
James; RG 7/3: 24, 529
RG 7/563: 15
Janfon; RG 7/3: 466
Janson; RG 7/3: 466
Jee; RG 7/3: 439
Jefferis; RG 7/3: 441
Jenings; RG 7/3: 173
Jenkins; RG 7/3: 33, 100,
336
Jenkinson; RG 7/3: 654
Jervis; RG 7/3: 631, 638
Jettur; RG 7/163: 11
Jewell; RG 7/3: 24, 108
Johnson; RG 7/3: 33, 52,
131, 160, 358, 378,
609 RG 7/163: 17, 34,
56 RG 7/563: 95, 160,
191
Johnstone; RG 7/3: 724 RG
7/563: 177
Jones; RG 7/3: 74, 129,
142, 196, 212, 221,
338, 493, 508, 529,
555, 556, 669 RG
7/163: 15, 41, 63, 80,
95 RG 7/563: 41, 42,
196, 205
Jordan; RG 7/3: 423
Jorden; RG 7/3: 681
Jorney; RG 7/163: 30
Judd; RG 7/3: 559 RG
7/563: 45
Jurdon; RG 7/3: 229
Juxton; RG 7/3: 92
Keat; RG 7/3: 144
Keaves; RG 7/3: 171
Keen; RG 7/3: 261 RG
7/163: 96
Keep; RG 7/163: 116
Keeth; RG 7/3: 375
Kelham; RG 7/3: 502
Kelley; RG 7/3: 276
Kelshew; RG 7/3: 563 RG

7/563: 49
Kemp; RG 7/563: 140
Kennard; RG 7/163: 45
Kent; RG 7/3: 180, 194
Ketchmy; RG 7/3: 322
Ketham; RG 7/3: 502
Kewarden; RG 7/3: 510
Key; RG 7/3: 519, 706 RG
  7/563: 5
Killing; RG 7/3: 476
Kindell; RG 7/3: 641
King; RG 7/3: 74, 459,
  545 RG 7/163: 16 RG
  7/563: 31, 122
Kingham; RG 7/3: 372
Kington; RG 7/3: 145
Kinnion; RG 7/163: 104
Kirby; RG 7/3: 420
Kitchner; RG 7/563: 64
Kite; RG 7/3: 6
Kniblet; RG 7/563: 145
Knight; RG 7/3: 242, 295
  RG 7/163: 24
Kyrk; RG 7/163: 28
Lambert; RG 7/3: 549 RG
  7/563: 35
Lambkin; RG 7/163: 6
Lamy; RG 7/163: 32
Lane; RG 7/3: 84, 298,
  362, 624 RG 7/563: 116
Langley; RG 7/3: 13, 231,
  344
Langvile; RG 7/3: 408
Lansdale; RG 7/3: 541 RG
  7/563: 27
Lark; RG 7/3: 607, 662 RG
  7/563: 93
Larru; RG 7/163: 84
Latchman; RG 7/3: 151
Lathum; RG 7/3: 690
Latter; RG 7/3: 579 RG
  7/563: 66
Lattic; RG 7/3: 579
Laughlin; RG 7/3: 566 RG
  7/563: 52
Lavington; RG 7/3: 417
Lawalley; RG 7/3: 608 RG
  7/563: 94
Lawe; RG 7/3: 141
Lawrance; RG 7/563: 162
Lawrence; RG 7/3: 50, 679
Lawrenson; RG 7/3: 327

Lawson; RG 7/3: 239
Lea; RG 7/563: 137, 164,
  187
Leak; RG 7/3: 653 RG
  7/563: 158
Lee; RG 7/3: 546, 555 RG
  7/163: 88 RG 7/563: 32,
  41
Leeking; RG 7/3: 11
Leigh; RG 7/163: 58
Leonard; RG 7/3: 220 RG
  7/563: 182
Lethahir; RG 7/3: 173
Lettenbirg; RG 7/563: 136
Leveridg; RG 7/563: 28
Leveridge; RG 7/3: 542
Leweas; RG 7/163: 482
Lewgar; RG 7/3: 312
Lewin; RG 7/3: 481
Lewis; RG 7/3: 50 RG
  7/563: 202
Lewson; RG 7/563: 129
Lindeman; RG 7/163: 53
Linsey; RG 7/163: 10
Lintell; RG 7/3: 710
Linton; RG 7/3: 637
Linvel; RG 7/3: 487
Lions; RG 7/3: 109
Lipscombe; RG 7/3: 652
  RG 7/563: 157
Littleton; RG 7/163: 22
Lock; RG 7/3: 161
Lockey; RG 7/3: 263
Londer; RG 7/3: 453
Longbottom; RG 7/3: 56
Lording; RG 7/3: 4
Loton; RG 7/3: 629
Love; RG 7/3: 345
Low; RG 7/3: 319 RG
  7/163: 97 RG 7/563:
  143
Loxley; RG 7/3: 295
Loyd; RG 7/3: 9, 709
Loystom; RG 7/3: 34
Lucas; RG 7/3: 248, 548
  RG 7/563: 34, 101
Luis; RG 7/3: 125
Luke; RG 7/3: 283
Lutwich; RG 7/563: 109
Lynsey; RG 7/3: 557 RG
  7/563: 43
Lyon; RG 7/163: 74

Macdannal; RG 7/3: 479
Mackbeth; RG 7/3: 500
Mackphedre; RG 7/163: 24
Mackulla; RG 7/3: 464
Macneil; RG 7/163: 59
Maiden; RG 7/3: 310
Main; RG 7/3: 409
Mallard; RG 7/3: 238
Mallash; RG 7/3: 308
Mallery; RG 7/3: 196
Man; RG 7/3: 198
Manby; RG 7/3: 170
Mann; RG 7/163: 89
Manning; RG 7/3: 197 RG
  7/163: 76
Manthurst; RG 7/3: 436
Manton; RG 7/163: 54
Mardell; RG 7/163: 42
Mares; RG 7/563: 196
Margin; RG 7/3: 342
Markland; RG 7/3: 407
Marks; RG 7/3: 369, 524
  RG 7/563: 10
Marley; RG 7/3: 650
Marlow; RG 7/3: 437
Marriott; RG 7/3: 145, 682
Marsh; RG 7/563: 176
Marshall; RG 7/3: 58, 191
  RG 7/163: 9
Martin; RG 7/3: 246, 315,
  343, 554, 591, 657,
  665 RG 7/163: 17 RG
  7/563: 40, 78, 186
Masey; RG 7/3: 209
Mason; RG 7/3: 65, 321,
  615 RG 7/163: 107 RG
  7/563: 64, 102
Masters; RG 7/3: 101
Matrin; RG 7/3: 3
Mathews; RG 7/3: 648
Mattocks; RG 7/3: 550 RG
  7/563: 36
May; RG 7/3: 5, 108, 660
  RG 7/563: 193
Mayhew; RG 7/3: 249,
  582 RG 7/563: 70
Maynard; RG 7/163: 86
Maze; RG 7/3: 321
McCarley; RG 7/163: 34
Mearley; RG 7/163: 34
Mears; RG 7/3: 465
Mecartey; RG 7/163: 56

Merriam; RG 7/3: 168
Merritt; RG 7/163: 28
Miares; RG 7/3: 577
Miars; RG 7/563: 63
Miers; RG 7/163: 73
Miles; RG 7/3: 569 RG
7/563: 55
Mills; RG 7/3: 70, 138,
141, 342, 422, 569
Milton; RG 7/563: 179
Mingo; RG 7/3: 280
Mishard; RG 7/3: 205
Mitchell; RG 7/3: 113,
259, 348
Mittchel; RG 7/563: 131
Mochlord; RG 7/3: 280
Mongomery; RG 7/3: 51
Monk; RG 7/3: 351
Monrow; RG 7/163: 37
Moore; RG 7/3: 57, 216,
224, 341, 348, 398 RG
7/163: 16, 57
Moran; RG 7/163: 35
Morgan; RG 7/3: 266, 314,
458, 503, 525 RG
7/563: 11, 185
Morgen; RG 7/3: 656 RG
7/163: 41
Morris; RG 7/3: 2, 44, 106,
111, 124, 492, 669,
684 RG 7/163: 3
Morton; RG 7/3: 245
Most; RG 7/3: 457
Mountague; RG 7/3: 64
Mountain; RG 7/3: 640
Mountgomery; RG 7/163:
48
Mouth; RG 7/3: 665
Moyes; RG 7/163: 80
Moynard; RG 7/3: 293
Muckelroy; RG 7/3: 647
Muggleston; RG 7/3: 472
Mullely; RG 7/163: 102
Mullet; RG 7/3: 214 RG
7/163: 92
Munck; RG 7/3: 4
Munday; RG 7/3: 341, 623
Munjon; RG 7/3: 525
Munk; RG 7/3: 477
Munyon; RG 7/3: 525 RG
7/563: 11
Murfit; RG 7/3: 547 RG

7/563: 33
Murphu; RG 7/3: 470
Murphy; RG 7/3: 470, 694
Murry; RG 7/3: 453
Muscorey; RG 7/3: 316
Nailes; RG 7/3: 316
Naylor; RG 7/3: 175
Nele; RG 7/3: 495
Nettleship; RG 7/563: 190
Nevill; RG 7/3: 12, 136
Newberry; RG 7/3: 725 RG
7/563: 178
Newbury; RG 7/3: 159,
467
Newman; RG 7/3: 479
Nichol; RG 7/3: 195
Nichols; RG 7/3: 23, 642
RG 7/563: 124, 167
Nicholson; RG 7/3: 53
Nickol; RG 7/3: 8
Nisler; RG 7/3: 288
Nixon; RG 7/3: 285
Nock; RG 7/3: 329
Normand; RG 7/163: 20
Norris; RG 7/3: 175, 425
North; RG 7/3: 1
Norton; RG 7/163: 117
Norway; RG 7/3: 269
Norwich; RG 7/3: 627
Nuts; RG 7/3: 570 RG
7/563: 56
Obbs; RG 7/563: 183
Obrian; RG 7/3: 452
Ogle; RG 7/3: 567 RG
7/563: 53
Oliver; RG 7/3: 429
Ollerhead; RG 7/3: 627
Ollford; RG 7/163: 119
Oneel; RG 7/563: 111
Oram; RG 7/3: 538 RG
7/563: 24
Orpwood; RG 7/163: 78
Orton; RG 7/3: 405, 654
RG 7/563: 167
Osband; RG 7/3: 674
Osborn; RG 7/3: 182
Oswald; RG 7/3: 72
Oswyn; RG 7/3: 119
Owens; RG 7/3: 266
Oxlad; RG 7/3: 655
Pain; RG 7/3: 306
Paine; RG 7/3: 667

Painter; RG 7/563: 119
Pallet; RG 7/3: 512
Palmer; RG 7/3: 264, 414,
698
Panton; RG 7/3: 218
Par; RG 7/563: 113
Paris; RG 7/3: 663
Parker; RG 7/163: 40
Parkines; RG 7/3: 5
Parkins; RG 7/3: 523 RG
7/563: 9
Parrat; RG 7/3: 427
Parris; RG 7/3: 526 RG
7/563: 12
Parry; RG 7/163: 29
Parson; RG 7/3: 689
Parsons; RG 7/3: 643
Partridge; RG 7/163: 73
Patrick; RG 7/3: 661
Patten; RG 7/3: 396
Peace; RG 7/563: 144
Pearce; RG 7/3: 217 RG
7/563: 169
Pearpoint; RG 7/3: 98
Pearre; RG 7/3: 705
Pears; RG 7/3: 14
Pedley; RG 7/163: 21
Peeke; RG 7/3: 269
Peers; RG 7/3: 397
Peirce; RG 7/3: 142, 180
RG 7/163: 101
Pell; RG 7/3: 210
Penn; RG 7/3: 330
Perkins; RG 7/3: 523
Perring; RG 7/3: 601 RG
7/563: 88
Pescott; RG 7/3: 527 RG
7/563: 13
Peterson; RG 7/163: 19
Pett; RG 7/163: 1
Petterson; RG 7/3: 398
Pettit; RG 7/3: 429
Petts; RG 7/163: 83
Pewtris; RG 7/3: 563 RG
7/563: 49
Peyton; RG 7/163: 70
Phillips; RG 7/3: 118, 150,
355, 444
Phillpot; RG 7/163: 66
Phipps; RG 7/3: 228, 346
Phipson; RG 7/3: 265
Phrasier; RG 7/3: 193

115

Pickman; RG 7/3: 666
Pictman; RG 7/3: 666
Pilgram; RG 7/563: 137
Pink; RG 7/563: 1
Pinsin; RG 7/3: 252
Pinson; RG 7/3: 366
Pironie; RG 7/3: 625
Pitt; RG 7/3: 507 RG
 7/163: 101
Pitts; RG 7/3: 230, 343,
 347
Place; RG 7/3: 48
Plan; RG 7/3: 699
Plasteed; RG 7/3: 140
Platt; RG 7/3: 236, 239
Platts; RG 7/3: 377
Plaw; RG 7/3: 267
Plowman; RG 7/563: 173
Plumer; RG 7/3: 387
Plummer; RG 7/3: 375
Pollet; RG 7/3: 512
Porter; RG 7/3: 104 RG
 7/163: 45
Posmore; RG 7/163: 49
Potter; RG 7/3: 664 RG
 7/163: 87
Pottle; RG 7/563: 144
Poulton; RG 7/3: 374
Pouttney; RG 7/3: 430
Powell; RG 7/3: 100, 114,
 419
Pratt; RG 7/3: 42, 400
Preist; RG 7/3: 411
Pressland; RG 7/563: 163
Prestwood; RG 7/3: 433
Price; RG 7/3: 169, 226
 RG 7/163: 52 RG 7/563:
 130
Prichard; RG 7/3: 258,
 714
Pricktoe; RG 7/563: 128
Pritchard; RG 7/3: 132
Procter; RG 7/3: 62, 232
Prosser; RG 7/3: 202
Pue; RG 7/3: 689
Pumer; RG 7/3: 687
Purson; RG 7/3: 236
Pynsent; RG 7/3: 366
Ragg; RG 7/3: 350
Ramsey; RG 7/563: 168
Rash; RG 7/3: 523 RG
 7/563: 9

Ratlife; RG 7/3: 47
Rawlings; RG 7/3: 21, 189
Rawlingson; RG 7/3: 44
Read; RG 7/3: 257
Readen; RG 7/3: 521
Reader; RG 7/3: 521 RG
 7/563: 7
Reason; RG 7/563: 195
Redfarn; RG 7/3: 154
Redframe; RG 7/3: 356
Redhead; RG 7/3: 612 RG
 7/563: 98
Redman; RG 7/3: 374
Reed; RG 7/3: 572 RG
 7/563: 58
Reeves; RG 7/3: 82
Regnier; RG 7/163: 8
Reich; RG 7/563: 30
Ren; RG 7/563: 135
Rennolds; RG 7/3: 723 RG
 7/563: 144, 180
Rennolls; RG 7/3: 399
Reve; RG 7/3: 618 RG
 7/563: 106
Revell; RG 7/3: 390
Reyner; RG 7/3: 415
Reynolds; RG 7/3: 81, 83,
 121, 639 RG 7/163: 9,
 66
Reynoldson; RG 7/3: 17
Rich; RG 7/3: 544 RG
 7/563: 153
Richard; RG 7/3: 149
Richards; RG 7/3: 61, 251,
 354, 719
Richardson; RG 7/3: 156,
 469, 530, 560, 587 RG
 7/163: 58, 114 RG
 7/563: 16, 46, 74, 138
Riches; RG 7/3: 247
Ridgment; RG 7/3: 290
Riggs; RG 7/163: 83
Right; RG 7/3: 92, 116
Riley; RG 7/163: 104
Riter; RG 7/163: 109
Riveres; RG 7/3: 691
Rivet; RG 7/3: 434
Roberts; RG 7/3: 118,
 385, 403, 431 RG
 7/163: 46 RG 7/563:
 130
Robertson; RG 7/3: 599 RG

7/563: 86
Robetson; RG 7/563: 86
Robinson; RG 7/3: 20, 45,
 265
Rodgers; RG 7/3: 255,
 273, 326
Rofeer; RG 7/3: 547 RG
 7/563: 33
Rogers; RG 7/3: 423
Rolles; RG 7/3: 701
Ross; RG 7/3: 223
Roteer; RG 7/563: 33
Rotherham; RG 7/3: 718
Rotledge; RG 7/3: 376
Round; RG 7/3: 494
Rouse; RG 7/3: 602
Row; RG 7/163: 110
Rowe; RG 7/3: 677
Rowel; RG 7/3: 485
Rowland; RG 7/163: 99
Rowse; RG 7/563: 89
Royston; RG 7/3: 12
Rudson; RG 7/563: 126
Ruslon; RG 7/3: 620
Russell; RG 7/3: 69, 129
Rutter; RG 7/163: 94
Rylan; RG 7/563: 172
Rylands; RG 7/3: 415
Sadler; RG 7/3: 113
Sample; RG 7/3: 91, 134
Sandall; RG 7/3: 442
Sanders; RG 7/3: 382,
 560, 684, 688 RG
 7/563: 46
Sandys; RG 7/163: 84
Saner; RG 7/3: 334
Saunders; RG 7/3: 551,
 560 RG 7/563: 37
Savage; RG 7/3: 241, 605
 RG 7/563: 92, 175
Sawyer; RG 7/3: 331, 539
 RG 7/563: 25
Scarfe; RG 7/3: 235
Scomb; RG 7/3: 595 RG
 7/563: 82
Scrooby; RG 7/3: 36
Seager; RG 7/3: 410
Seaton; RG 7/3: 66, 170
Secomb; RG 7/3: 595 RG
 7/563: 82
Sedwick; RG 7/3: 606
Selbey; RG 7/3: 1

Sells; RG 7/3: 499
Sexton; RG 7/3: 66
Shard; RG 7/3: 112
Sharp; RG 7/3: 462
Sharwood; RG 7/3: 715
Shaw; RG 7/3: 38, 63,
473, 592, 602 RG
7/563: 79, 89, 147
Sheepherd; RG 7/563: 174
Shelton; RG 7/563: 126
Shepard; RG 7/3: 167, 359
RG 7/563: 202
Shepherd; RG 7/563: 174,
192
Sheppard; RG 7/3: 318 RG
7/563: 148
Shevers; RG 7/3: 48
Shippey; RG 7/3: 124
Shipton; RG 7/3: 15
Short; RG 7/3: 70, 109,
331
Shuter; RG 7/3: 272
Silkwood; RG 7/3: 513
Simison; RG 7/163: 69
Simmonds; RG 7/163: 12
Simmons; RG 7/3: 403,
535 RG 7/563: 21
Simms; RG 7/3: 207
Simpkin; RG 7/3: 27
Simpson; RG 7/3: 78, 275,
317, 531, 635, 680 RG
7/563: 17, 112
Sinclair; RG 7/3: 171
Singclear; RG 7/3: 171
Skinner; RG 7/563: 133
Sleigh; RG 7/563: 151
Slough; RG 7/563: 151
Sloughton; RG 7/3: 442
Sly; RG 7/3: 167, 359
Small; RG 7/3: 406, 582
RG 7/163: 72 RG 7/563:
70
Smallbones; RG 7/3: 97
Smart; RG 7/3: 2, 338
Smith; RG 7/3: 3, 176,
219, 237, 244, 270,
360, 362, 394, 405,
421, 491, 562, 585,
609, 617, 633, 712,
713 RG 7/163: 72 RG
7/563: 48, 72, 95, 105,
149, 199

Snape; RG 7/163: 30
Snelling; RG 7/3: 153
Snow; RG 7/163: 78
Sommers; RG 7/3: 222
Song; RG 7/3: 558
Songhurst; RG 7/3: 272
Southern; RG 7/3: 226
Southhall; RG 7/563: 193
Southwell; RG 7/3: 44
Sowden; RG 7/3: 287
Soyer; RG 7/3: 337
Sozer; RG 7/3: 257
Sparkes; RG 7/3: 692
Speed; RG 7/3: 645
Spencer; RG 7/3: 128,
422, 670 RG 7/163: 23
RG 7/563: 198
Spurham; RG 7/3: 589 RG
7/563: 76
Stacey; RG 7/3: 364
Stack; RG 7/163: 107
Staffes; RG 7/3: 427
Stafford; RG 7/3: 294
Standwick; RG 7/3: 465
Staner; RG 7/3: 565
Stanes; RG 7/3: 565 RG
7/563: 51
Stanley; RG 7/3: 204, 529
RG 7/563: 15, 129
Staple; RG 7/3: 253
Staples; RG 7/3: 484
Statchberry; RG 7/563:
197
Stears; RG 7/3: 181
Steed; RG 7/3: 201 RG
7/163: 77
Steel; RG 7/3: 412
Steele; RG 7/3: 64
Steinfels; RG 7/163: 109
Stennett; RG 7/3: 652 RG
7/563: 157
Stephens; RG 7/3: 372,
548 RG 7/563: 34, 206
Stephenson; RG 7/3: 325
Stepple; RG 7/163: 95
Stevens; RG 7/3: 133,
284, 324, 637
Steward; RG 7/3: 104, 167
Stewdly; RG 7/3: 650
Stiles; RG 7/3: 561 RG
7/563: 47
Stone; RG 7/3: 527 RG

7/563: 13, 129
Stowell; RG 7/3: 96
Straford; RG 7/3: 593
Stratford; RG 7/3: 593 RG
7/563: 80
Stredwick; RG 7/563: 123
Street; RG 7/3: 681
Strong; RG 7/3: 25
Strowd; RG 7/563: 142
Stuard; RG 7/3: 409
Sugg; RG 7/3: 449
Swain; RG 7/3: 254
Swallow; RG 7/3: 455
Swarbrick; RG 7/163: 35
Sweet; RG 7/3: 278
Sweeting; RG 7/3: 515,
628 RG 7/563: 2
Sweetman; RG 7/3: 519
Swenland; RG 7/3: 537,
576
Swenleman; RG 7/3: 489
Swercand; RG 7/3: 708
Sweret; RG 7/3: 571 RG
7/563: 57
Swetman; RG 7/3: 519,
706 RG 7/563: 5
Swezland; RG 7/3: 537 RG
7/563: 23, 62
Swift; RG 7/3: 144
Symble; RG 7/3: 46
Symonds; RG 7/3: 32
Syms; RG 7/3: 470 RG
7/563: 110, 113
Talbot; RG 7/3: 457
Talbott; RG 7/3: 191
Tallcott; RG 7/3: 418
Tanner; RG 7/3: 456, 516,
630
Taplis; RG 7/563: 154
Tappey; RG 7/163: 29
Tapping; RG 7/3: 101
Tate; RG 7/3: 497
Tather; RG 7/163: 19
Tatlock; RG 7/3: 160, 358
Tayler; RG 7/3: 612, 672,
685
Taylor; RG 7/3: 39, 162,
262, 267, 369, 452 RG
7/163: 33, 70, 81, 86
RG 7/563: 98, 184
Tearley; RG 7/163: 99
Temple; RG 7/3: 339

Templeman; RG 7/163: 103
Templet; RG 7/3: 450
Terwin; RG 7/163: 103
Thavane; RG 7/163: 67
Thirft; RG 7/3: 206
Thirst; RG 7/3: 206
Thomarver; RG 7/3: 539 RG 7/563: 25
Thomas; RG 7/3: 379, 438 RG 7/563: 149, 172
Thompson; RG 7/3: 536, 635, 702 RG 7/563: 22
Thomson; RG 7/3: 120, 126
Thornboroughs; RG 7/163: 14
Throsley; RG 7/3: 667
Tigan; RG 7/3: 491
Tippett; RG 7/563: 114
Tipping; RG 7/163: 39
Tod; RG 7/3: 447
Tolett; RG 7/3: 351
Tompson; RG 7/3: 289
Tong; RG 7/3: 558 RG 7/563: 44
Toplift; RG 7/563: 121
Torrington; RG 7/3: 469
Townsend; RG 7/3: 282
Tranter; RG 7/163: 81
Treacher; RG 7/563: 141
Treasure; RG 7/3: 443
Tredwell; RG 7/3: 34
Tribe; RG 7/3: 179
Trotter; RG 7/3: 400
Truby; RG 7/3: 40, 80
Trudgion; RG 7/3: 214
Trueman; RG 7/3: 662
Truso; RG 7/3: 75
Tubb; RG 7/163: 69
Tuder; RG 7/3: 475
Turbel; RG 7/3: 212
Turf; RG 7/563: 127
Turlington; RG 7/3: 713
Turner; RG 7/3: 162, 352, 387, 399, 424, 516, 621, 658 RG 7/563: 3, 132, 165
Turvey; RG 7/163: 65
Twitchen; RG 7/563: 190
Twist; RG 7/3: 72
Tyday; RG 7/3: 432

Ufford; RG 7/3: 596 RG 7/563: 83
Umber; RG 7/563: 107
Umfrevill; RG 7/163: 36
Underwood; RG 7/3: 105, 149, 354, 543 RG 7/563: 29
Urlin; RG 7/3: 128
Uthwait; RG 7/3: 71
Uxley; RG 7/3: 11
Vaudery; RG 7/563: 117
Vaughan; RG 7/3: 633
Vawdrey; RG 7/163: 18
Veal; RG 7/3: 159
Verey; RG 7/3: 382
Vernon; RG 7/163: 55
Vesey; RG 7/3: 281
Vincent; RG 7/3: 14, 84 RG 7/563: 197
Vinsent; RG 7/3: 84
Virent; RG 7/3: 363
Vopalter; RG 7/3: 304
Wadley; RG 7/563: 194
Waine; RG 7/3: 716
Waite; RG 7/163: 79
Wakeford; RG 7/3: 539 RG 7/563: 25
Waker; RG 7/563: 22
Waklin; RG 7/3: 568 RG 7/563: 54
Walhen; RG 7/3: 459
Walher; RG 7/3: 336
Walken; RG 7/3: 459
Walker; RG 7/3: 247, 336, 377, 448, 475, 536, 605, 711 RG 7/563: 92, 188
Walkin; RG 7/3: 568
Wall; RG 7/3: 219, 562 RG 7/563: 48
Want; RG 7/563: 155
Ward; RG 7/3: 90, 543, 697 RG 7/563: 29
Ware; RG 7/3: 63
Warne; RG 7/3: 147
Warner; RG 7/3: 618 RG 7/563: 106
Warren; RG 7/163: 31
Warrin; RG 7/3: 660
Warsar; RG 7/3: 694
Warwick; RG 7/3: 223, 668

Water; RG 7/3: 714
Waterman; RG 7/163: 6
Waters; RG 7/3: 121, 271, 597 RG 7/563: 84
Watkins; RG 7/3: 133 RG 7/563: 132
Watman; RG 7/3: 646
Watson; RG 7/3: 73, 203, 481
Watts; RG 7/563: 109
Wattson; RG 7/3: 75, 91, 99, 235
Wayland; RG 7/3: 682
Wear; RG 7/563: 165
Weaver; RG 7/3: 677
Webb; RG 7/3: 89, 371 RG 7/163: 25
Webber; RG 7/3: 379
Webbster; RG 7/3: 224
Webster; RG 7/163: 18
Weeble; RG 7/163: 5
Weiden; RG 7/3: 695
Weld; RG 7/163: 36
Welle; RG 7/163: 68
Wells; RG 7/3: 454
Wentworth; RG 7/3: 608 RG 7/563: 94
West; RG 7/3: 645, 666 RG 7/563: 152
Westid; RG 7/3: 692
Westobey; RG 7/3: 41
Westwood; RG 7/563: 181
Wever; RG 7/563: 161
Wharff; RG 7/3: 238
Wharton; RG 7/3: 553 RG 7/563: 39
Wheeler; RG 7/163: 25
Wherlow; RG 7/3: 268
Whiler; RG 7/3: 687
White; RG 7/3: 47, 111, 208, 361, 388, 613 RG 7/563: 99
Whitecoat; RG 7/3: 588 RG 7/563: 75
Whitehead; RG 7/3: 88, 213, 521 RG 7/563: 7
Whiteman; RG 7/3: 487
Whitlock; RG 7/3: 55
Whitrell; RG 7/3: 279
Whyte; RG 7/163: 47
Whyvell; RG 7/3: 683
Wicks; RG 7/3: 222

Wiggin; RG 7/3: 127
Wiley; RG 7/163: 76
Wiliams; RG 7/3: 705
Wilkins; RG 7/3: 87
Wilkinson; RG 7/3: 260
Wilks; RG 7/3: 463
Willbrame; RG 7/163: 75
Willcox; RG 7/163: 89 RG
7/563: 67, 103
Willdam; RG 7/3: 554 RG
7/563: 40
Williams; RG 7/3: 18, 154,
189, 197, 227, 356,
424, 528, 545, 617,
722 RG 7/163: 94 RG
7/563: 14, 31, 105,
136, 141
Willmer; RG 7/163: 19
Willmoth; RG 7/3: 619 RG
7/563: 204
Wills; RG 7/163: 106
Willson; RG 7/3: 130, 483,
540, 587, 703 RG
7/163: 88 RG 7/563: 26
Wilmot; RG 7/3: 122
Wilson; RG 7/3: 335 RG
7/163: 5 RG 7/563: 74
Winch; RG 7/3: 183
Winton; RG 7/3: 478
Winwood; RG 7/3: 421
Wisdon; RG 7/3: 59
Witall; RG 7/3: 663
Witney; RG 7/3: 530 RG
7/563: 16
Wolford; RG 7/3: 436
Wood; RG 7/3: 28, 32,
250, 297, 446, 526,
540, 673, 703 RG
7/163: 90, 115 RG
7/563: 12, 26
Woodcock; RG 7/563:
131, 171
Woodham; RG 7/3: 651 RG
7/563: 156
Woodhead; RG 7/3: 622
Woodin; RG 7/3: 699
Woodland; RG 7/3: 700
Woofatt; RG 7/163: 47
Wooten; RG 7/3: 693
Worril; RG 7/3: 593 RG
7/563: 80
Wright; RG 7/3: 7, 193,

260, 314, 373, 447,
460 RG 7/563: 181
Wyatt; RG 7/3: 127
Wyment; RG 7/3: 715
Yardley; RG 7/3: 198
Yeomans; RG 7/3: 721
Yexley; RG 7/163: 43
Yonge; RG 7/3: 675
Youll; RG 7/163: 85
Young; RG 7/3: 243, 335,
365 RG 7/163: 57, 71
Younger; RG 7/563: 108